By Sabrina Mesko

Healing Mudras: Yoga for Your Hands – original edition
POWER MUDRAS: Yoga Hand Postures for Women
Mudras for the ZODIAC: Volume I. – XII.
Healing Mudras I. – For Your Body
Healing Mudras II. - For Your Mind
Healing Mudras III. – For Your Soul
Chakra Mudras DVD set
HEALING MUDRAS Yoga for Your Hands - New Edition
MUDRA THERAPY – Hand Yoga for Pain Management and Conquering Illness

YOGA MIND

45 MEDITATIONS
For INNER PEACE, PROSPERITY
and PROTECTION

By Sabrina Mesko Ph.D.H.

The material contained in this book has been written for informational purposes and is not intended as a substitute for medical advice nor is it intended to diagnose, treat, cure, or prevent disease. If you have a medical issue or illness, consult a qualified physician.

A Mudra Hands™ Book
Published by Mudra Hands Publishing

Photography by Sabrina Mesko, Kiar Mesko
Illustrations by Kiar Mesko
Cover photo by Rafael Marn
Cover and interior book design by Sabrina Mesko
Printed in the United States of America

ISBN-13: 978-0615891200
ISBN-10: 0615891209

For my Father Kiar

and all He continues to teach me

about the Mystery of the Mind

TABLE OF CONTENTS

YOGA MIND

45 MEDITATIONS

For Inner Peace, Prosperity and Protection

Introduction

I believe that the power of our mind is the most unexplored and underestimated power available to us. Each one of us obviously has a mind, but not everyone knows how to use it to it's full potential. The ones that do, are light years ahead of the rest, who are left behind feeling helpless and powerless.

Nobody said it was easy or effortless to achieve a state of piece in your mind, but it is absolutely possible.

To be able to still, focus and direct your mind to where it can create a positive change in your life: that means you have learned to truly use something you were born with. Regardless of how gifted or intelligent you are, you have the capacity to achieve control of the power of your mind. When your mind is properly understood and activated, you become an active participant and co-creator of your life, as opposed to just and observer, watching and waiting in fear and helpless anticipation what may come your way. I am here to remind you of that fact and show you a hopeful and optimistic way out of the haze of everyday life where you may feel overwhelmed and hopeless. I believe that you can consciously change your mindset and thus your life.

It is all about practice and mind exercise.

Training your mind to obey your direction takes discipline and work.

But it can be incredibly adventurous, exciting and definitely fun.

The end result is beyond rewarding. It is simply life altering.

Every day presents a new beginning, new opportunity for a new experience.

No matter how restricting the life circumstances you are facing seem to be, your mental disposition in conquering a challenge plays a key role. Your inner dialogue is your constant companion - cheering you on or dragging you down.

Are we truly aware of the crucial effect of our inner dialogue?

It all begins in your mind.

Do you want to be open to new possibilities for a happier more fulfilled life?

Are you stuck in old mind pattern and can't seem to dig yourself out?

You always have an option, a choice:

do you move forward or leave things as they are?

Even if everything that surrounds you seems to be at a standstill, your mind is always free. You can rethink, visualize, create and imagine a positive conclusion to any problem you may be facing…and again, it all starts in your mind.

The true astonishing power of our mind is still undiscovered. Speculations that we use only 10% of the brain is merely guessing which leads us to believe that perhaps we only understand 10% of the brain.

Leaving the scientific discussions aside, one thing is however clear: there are undiscovered, unknown and mysterious facts surrounding our brainpower and our mind. The power of one's thought is definitely a force to be reckoned with, like an energy signal that creates a ripple effect of un-tangible proportions.

We have all experienced the almost spooky quality of mind reception and uttered words like "You just read my mind" or perhaps "I was thinking the exactly same thing". But how can you explain this mysterious occurrence?

The power of our mind is beyond fascinating. It is absolutely mysterious, magical and almost frightening. We humans often fear what we don't understand, can't see or touch.

But think about the ever-present thoughts, the visual explorations of our future possible events and the amazing effect our inner dialogue has on our life. It is timeless, limitless and allows us to travel wherever we want without time, space, comfort or budget limitations.

To me, this has always presented an incredible fascination and challenge.

I remember as a child wanting to understand everything: why are there stars in the sky, where do the galaxies end, how to travel thru time, or visit the different dimensions, other intelligence, what were the secrets of the mysterious Egyptian past and all the magical possibilities of the future. I would think about it for hours and could not find peace until I came up with some sort of acceptable explanation provided either by my father, some reasonable self-made theory or a selection of books. My father who is a deeply spiritual artist and was an art professor, always patiently answered my most intricate and never ending questions. He also left much space for my own inner reflexion and subsequent conclusions. Discussions with him did not simply provide an answer, but challenged me to explore further into my subconscious and search for an answer within my own intuition, logical thinking and of course plenty of imagination with it. More often than not, his answer was to pose me a question in return and that prompted me to search deeply within for possible answers.

In the many years since then, I continue my discussions with him and they remain equally fascinating to me, but obviously deeper, more complex and intricate. Most of the time we laugh and agree how little we humans really know. I feel incredibly fortunate and grateful to have him in my life.

My life has presented me with unique opportunities to personally meet various true yoga Masters from India, and I have always enthusiastically asked them every possible question about the power of the mind. Some answers were astonishing and I still can't wrap my mind around them. But as expected, thru the years my knowledge has expanded and ripened. With time, life has brought me many challenges, difficult transitions, profound changes, gains and deep looses, but everything that I have experiences so far has brought me even deeper conviction and realization how important and crucial a positive mind set is. That is why thru it all, I still consider myself an extraordinarily lucky individual. I remain an optimist and always strive to see a glimmer of good even in the darkest of hours. This belief has gotten me thru most amazingly challenging and exhausting life's journeys. It was with the power of my positive mindset and focused vision of a victorious outcome that I remained steady on course and conquered the seemingly helpless circumstances.

Life taught me and proved again and again that the power of mind truly works and how indescribably important it is to be conscious of our every thought, mind projection and our future that we envision.

Let's not forget that side by side with the technique of visualization, we must nurture and master the capacity to remain open and receptive to the thoughts, ideas and answers that freely come our way when needed.

The inner voice must be heard for it holds all the answers.

How can we find it, this all knowing and wise, inner teacher?

YOGA FOR YOUR MIND is most definitely a fantastic way to get there.

It takes a disciplined conscious practice and deep inner search to embrace the journey of self-discovery. Once you understand and know Yourself, the seemingly cluttered mind disappears and a new, open, receptive and guiding inner voice emerges. Clearing your mind and making space for the new You, the empowered You, the wise, patient and enlightened You.

I would like to remind you that the learning curve of life never ends and there is no finishing chapter, where we can say that "now, we know it all".

We don't and we won't and that is the beauty of it.

Yoga has become incredibly popular and everybody seems to be familiar with the basic aspect of yoga and it's various physical exercises and techniques.

Of course meditation is an intricate part of yoga and the millions of people that mediate daily experience and embrace the importance of mind stillness.

I do wonder, how many of us truly enjoy the full benefit of the mind stillness after Hatha yoga or meditation practice. Of course we are aware that we experience a physical sense of peace, harmony and increased energy level after yoga practice, but do we truly relish and fully enjoy the stillness and inner peace that we just begin to experience in our mind at that particular point? Even loyal meditation practitioners need time to experience peace with the help of practice of various meditation techniques, but when true stillness of the mind is achieved, do they explore this journey further and open their mind to creative inner dialogue? Do they consciously direct their mind to explore possible future life circumstances? Do they actively participate in co-creating their future? Or are they content with the inner peace and stillness and consider that the final goal? Disciplined yoga and meditation practitioners experience and understand the peace, serenity, renewed energy level and joy after a regular practice routine. But I do believe that more often than not, we don't take full advantage of this receptive and fruitful post -yoga - practice state we are in. Usually we rush off, busy with our schedules and eager to go on with our day. Life pushes us in this direction, time is always of the essence and in demand and there is never enough of it.

But what if we would take just a bit more time, stay put, and acknowledge the fact that we are just at the beginning of a deeper inner dialogue and search and that NOW presents a perfect opportunity to hear our mind, our thoughts, ask questions and actually get easy flowing insightful and inspiring answers?

I believe that adding the conscious visualization and inner communication exercises at the end of a regular yoga practice would be of tremendous benefit to all. I know some of you are on that path. Within the book you hold in your hands, you will find more options, a greater vocabulary of inner journeys with a specific focus and direction, to ease your way in self-discovery and help accelerate your journey to self-realization.

Yoga teaches us how we must first still the body, and then we can still the mind. More often than not, this is where it ends. We feel calmer, peaceful, enlightened and serene and I agree that is the basis for the next level of self-discovery.

How many of us realize that it is at this crucial point that one can begin to hear their inner voice and create a desired picture willingly and with true loving intention?

Being open to your own creative input is essentially important.

It presents the world of new possibilities, optimism and hope.

It provides answers to your deepest questions and possibly helps you recognize a new direction that leads you to a happier more fulfilled life.

It helps you remember your destined path.

May I remind you again, that to keep an open receptive mind takes work.

To visualize a successful positive outcome when challenged by an obstacle can be essentially life transforming.

That is what the true power of manifestation really is. It is not about obsessive control over everything. It is about accessing the field of endless possibilities, infusing them with a breath of life and knowing that you have truly done everything you can to help manifest the best optimal outcome desired. If you do your part well, the invisible energy will create a chain reaction and help move the wheels of destiny in such a way that the truly best outcome will manifest. It may be different from what you envisioned, but you will soon see, it will be even better. This way, you have actively participated in informing and signaling the universe your desire, your wish, your hope and the universe will respond accordingly. Trust it.

But all of this truly begins in your mind with the proper techniques to access it. Once you learn these techniques, they will come to you naturally and immediately. You won't need to go thru a rigorous physical exercise to reach the deeper level of peace of mind. You will be able to just find a moment of stillness instantly wherever you are, and connect to that inner control center that is always within reach. Your mind will become your anchor no matter what whirlwind and sand storm envelops you. You will hold it firmly, with unwavering strength and clear intention. Your life will change dramatically, your destined path will reveal itself and your sense of fulfillment will fill your heart and soul. You will finally feel at home here in this world. You will recognize it's distracting illusions and find a clear path thru foggy challenging forest of adventure. But most of all, your spirit will soar in content happiness and joy, knowing that you belong, you have a purpose and are in perfect harmony with the universe. That is invaluable and irreplaceable. You will experience a love of life, for yourself, for others and for that universal power that protects, loves and connects us all.

Awaken and enjoy the true potential of this life experience and I pray you use it only with loving, giving and peace inducing intention for it is only then that it will work. The unseen law of manifestation guards it's gates and manifests only when infused with the selfless purest of love and service. Knowing yourself, helping others and protecting our planet are your mantras on this journey. Fill it with compassion for yourself and others for we are on this journey together, now and always.

YOGA FOR YOUR MIND is the natural next step in our evolution of self-realization. Once we jointly embrace and breathe with the fearless understanding that time, space and love have not limits, we are ready to enter the new age of enlightenment and expanded consciousness.

I welcome you to this new inner journey and envision you happy, healthy, content with self empowerment, and inspired with universal love and supreme knowledge. May the newly discovered power of your mind take you there.

Blessings and peace,

Sabrina

PART ONE

Instructions for Practice

1. WHAT IS YOGA FOR YOUR MIND

Yoga is the union of body, mind and spirit with the One, the universal energy, ever-present force, the Creator or God.

Yoga is an indescribable ancient gift to us all. It offers a rich spectrum of ancient techniques that enable us to experience a truly revealing journey of self-discovery which ultimately brings us closer to self-realization and eventually to the One ever present Spirit.

There are many approaches and techniques to yoga practice and we each have to search for the one that suits our unique individual nature, personality, body, mind and spirit.

YOGA FOR YOUR MIND is a Western approach to an Eastern based Yoga technique called Raja Yoga.

Raja Yoga also known as "royal yoga", "royal union"or Classical Yoga.

These ancient teachings depict and cultivate the mind discipline by using mediation to achieve the final goal of liberation.

Raja Yoga – Yoga for Your Mind- is a practical guide for gaining control over your mind and actively creating and maintaining a positive mindset.

The ancient Indian scriptures tell us that our mind is considered to be the KING of our psycho-physical structure.

The mind and the body are of course interconnected and according to the yoga philosophy the body must be first disciplined through various physical techniques of Hatha yoga (physical yoga postures) and Pranayama (yogic breathing techniques) and with the help of a healthy lifestyle purified for good overall healthy state. The usual unhealthy distractions like addictions and obsessions prevent the practitioner from clear practice of meditation. Through self-discipline, restraint and abstinence from intoxicants, drugs and with conscious attention to healthy actions of body, speech and mind, a practitioner can prepare for a proper meditation practice. This mindful preparation and eventual disciplined practice of meditation evoke the desired results of deeper yoga experience.

For an individual to gain mastery over their mind is required great insight, patience, and skill. The mind is the most powerful force in all creation and the inner search, self-exploration, self-discipline, and deep inner awareness need guidance and explorative techniques to awaken this power within.

Once you experience that inter-connectedness, your life is forever positively transformed. Diminishing inner restlessness, unexplained dissatisfaction and seemingly permanent unhappy and unfulfilled state will transform and disappear when you discover that the true source of all your needs and the answers to your questions are truly within you.

Each one of us is given the capacity to experience that fulfilled state and contentment, the tangible happiness and joy, anytime and anyplace.

But we must consciously choose to do so, and diligently pursue that path towards self - realization.

The mind is like a wild horse running, torn between instinct, fear and desire. You can tame it, help it feel at peace, experience prosperous security and infinite protection. You are in charge, so take in the reigns and go where you want. **There are no limitations to your mind, it is as free as you let it be and as powerful as you allow it**. Manifest the life that you want by starting with the most needed change - the change in your mindset.

YOGA FOR YOUR MIND explores the unseen dimensions and layers to your mind power and encourages you not to focus solely on a singular desired object, but recognize and remove the endless old obstacles that live in your mind, clear the path for new patterns and thinking habits and introduce creative freedom into your new way of thinking. Within this experience you will find an opportunity to remain open to true universal Divinely guided inner voice, that will direct you exactly where you need to go. Once you recognize the power of your mind and use it, you will merge with your highest soul-potential-self and propel onto your life's true mission. The steps on this journey are challenging, but clear:

Mind stillness, focus and complete inner peace. The ancient scriptures teach us, that when with the help of meditation we achieve the spontaneous state of a truly quiet mind, we are considered to be at the starting point in the quest to cleanse our Karma (Cause and Effect) and attain Nirvana- ultimate bliss state.

I believe that in today's world with the big shifts that envelop us, we are in deep need for these techniques and also exceptionally fortunate when we are given clear tools to experience deep inner peace, create prosperity and assure our invincible protection. This way, we have everything we truly need in our lives.

2. HOW TO USE THIS BOOK

The techniques in this book are user friendly, adventurous and fun. They will propel you onto the most interesting and necessary journey of your life – the discovery of the power of your mind.

To practice these techniques you need just 30 minutes every other day. After reading a chapter and working thru the exercises, give your mind a day to absorb the new thought and have some needed space between new experiences.

The next day, review and repeat the exercise from the day before.

The following day, move forward to the next chapter.

In 12 weeks you will complete your work thru 45 chapters filled with techniques, exercises and tasks that will help you empower and understand the deeper levels - invisible dimensions of your being.

Read the chapter and practice the visualization exercise. An affirmation will follow to reestablish a new openness in your thinking patters. Each chapter ends with your journal work where you can reflect, search and discover the answers stored in your subconscious. You can practice these techniques anytime, but in the beginning it is helpful to have a peaceful and quiet area where you can completely relax.

After you become familiar with the inner journeys, you can practice them anywhere. When you are ready, your mind knows no boundaries and your intuition and awareness can be activated any place and any time.

3. INNER CONVERSATION

The Inner Conversation is your preparation for the Exercise. By reading or saying out loud the INNER CONVERSATION, you are opening and preparing your mind for a self-empowering information input. You are activating a positive energy current within you. Where your mind takes you every minute of the day has very strong consequences and literally directs your life. Let me give you a small example; let's say you feel like you're catching a cold. You have basically two options. You can give up and announce: "I am getting sick and feel terrible. The cold has got the best of me…"

Or, you realize your body is being challenged and is asking for your help.

In that case you could say: "A cold is trying to catch me, but I am doing everything I can, to stay healthy and prevent it as fast as possible. I know I can stay healthy." The difference in the attitude of your inner dialogue will influence how badly the cold will affect you. Your mind and emotions are involved in every aspect of your health, because it is YOUR mind, not separate from your body. Your mind is your command center therefore thoughts and words are powerful energy tools. Use them in a positive way and you will attract healthy power.

The INNER CONVERSATION will help you open your mind to the healing exercise-journey. It will help you focus and direct your mind into a state of peace, stillness and control, which will ultimately give you power over your mind. When you can control your mind and direct it to consciously create peace, health, protection and prosperity in your life, your life will dramatically change.

4.THE EXERCISE

The exercises are easy and fun self-discovering journeys with your mind. All you have to do is let your imagination and inner vision guide you thru the described visualization journey. Follow the instructions and let your mind take you there. You may start off with reading the exercise and visualizing as you go along. Once you become familiar with the exercise, you can take your time, close your eyes relax and really let go. The exercises are easy to remember. As always, your mind plays a very important role. Guide it and let your spiritual inner voice lead the way. Take your time and remember the experience, your feelings, questions and enlightening discoveries as you go along. Be attentive to your inner voice, a sensation, and a possible answer to your lingering question or a brand new idea. Remember, that no journey is the same, for each time your experience will reveal new and undiscovered places of your mind. You shall hear new guidance from your subconscious mind and higher wisdom from the deepest places of your soul.

5. AFFIRMATION

At the end of each visual journey exercise you will find an AFFIRMATION. After the exercise, your mind is receptive and open for the final positive self-empowering information input - a NEW WELLNESS CODE.

It will reaffirm your positive outlook and create new, self-empowering habits. Repeat the affirmation aloud or in your mind for at least a minute after the exercise. Remain still, absorb the affirmation and let it become a part of you. Enjoy the state of inner peace and power.

Your AFFIRMATION will seal the positive input.

6. YOUR JOURNAL

When you come to the last part of each chapter, you will find instructions for your JOURNAL notes. Keeping a journal will help your progress much faster. When we see the intentions and desires transformed into words, they take on another meaning. They become more powerful. On paper they already exist.

They made their way out of your mind into this dimension.

You may take notes, observations and keep track of the progress you've made. You will get a much clearer picture of what you've accomplished and where you want to go next. Your journal will prove very valuable and empowering on your journey towards inner peace, prosperity and protection. By writing your new discoveries, clear desires and goals into your journal and seeing them on paper, you are creating the first step in making them become your new desired reality.

7. THE RESULTS

It may seem simple at first, but with time you will discover the powerful meaning in your every thought. You will learn how to acknowledge and recognize those "coincidental moments" in your life where everything changes, makes sense and transforms your forever.

Awakening awareness and hearing your inner voice is most important for your happiness, fulfillment and a healthy heart.

This method will help you detach, remove and distance yourself from your everyday life where we tend forget why, where to and with whom.

There are reasons for every experience, good or bad, every relationship, love and every failure and success. You will be able to find and clear the path of your destined journey, approach the desired goal, experience happiness in simple moments and find the inner peace, prosperity, protection and the love you deserve. The search for your soul mate may be on, but the true search is really for your soul awareness. Once you remember who you are, what your dreams are and why you are here, everything will make sense, your true friends will appear and situations will develop with rapid speed where you will receive all the help you need to be on your way. Your true love is here, waiting for that perfect moment when you are both ready. But first remember to wake up, look around and learn to love yourself.

Your success awaits, but you need to recognize your destined path in order to pursue it. When your heart, mind and spirit are filled with peace, all else shall follow. Prosperity is within your reach when you are in tune with your true-life purpose. Protection is your birthright and by tangible awareness that we are all part of this universe you will attract and key into the universal protective power. Enjoy the journey and when ready, spread the peace all around you.

A peaceful world is something we all deserve, desire and are destined to live in. The universe will always help you. Just do your very best, listen to your inner voice and remain steady and strong. Keep the faith. We are all together at this predestined time. There is no moment like now. It is all that matters. And right now your life is ok, for you are reading this book and deep down inside you, you know very well that everything is going to be more than ok.

This is your life…right now …and you are doing great!

HEAL your PAST, PRESENT and FUTURE

8. YOUR CHAKRA MAP

First Chakra - Foundation & Vitality
Represents: Survival, food, shelter, courage, will, foundation
Location: Base of spine   **Color**: Red

Second Chakra - Sexuality & Creativity
Represents: Sex, creativity, procreation, family, inspiration
Location: Sex organs   **Color**: Orange

Third Chakra - Ego & Mind
Represents: Ego, emotional center, the intellect, the mind
Location: Solar plexus   **Color**: Yellow

Fourth Chakra - Love
Represents: Unconditional true love, devotion, faith, compassion
Location: heart region   **Color**: Green or pink

Fifth Chakra - Truth & Communication
Represents: Voice, truth, communication, higher knowledge
Location: Throat   **Color**: Blue

Sixth Chakra - Intuition
Represents: Third Eye, vision, intuition
Location: Third Eye   **Color**: Indigo

Seventh Chakra - Divine Wisdom
Represents: Universal God consciousness, the heavens, unity, humility
Location: Top of the head, crown **Color**: Violet

PART TWO

Peace in Your BODY

9. HEALING BREATH

The most important step towards health and a peaceful state of your body, mind and soul is proper breathing. You take your first breath when you come into this world and you exhale your last breath upon your departure. Breathing is an essential part of your life. How you breathe reveals a lot about your state of mind, your emotions, general health, personality and energy level. Proper breathing positively affects your overall health, lowers high blood pressure, releases stress, tension, and helps you eliminate toxins from the body while adding a healthy glow to your skin. When exercising, it is essential to breathe correctly, so that you may aid your body's natural ability to release toxins through exhalations.

Most of us don't breathe correctly. And yet, when you were a baby, your breathing was perfect. Have you ever observed a sleeping baby and its peaceful way of breathing? With each inhalation the stomach expands and with each exhalation the stomach relaxes. That is the correct way to breathe. We tend to breathe exactly the opposite way. What happened? With years of stress, anxiety, and fears, we tighten and close up the stomach area, which needs to stay relaxed. We forget how to properly breathe and leave little room for vital healing energy to enter our body. But the good news is, that you can easily remind and re-train yourself back to that healthy way of breathing.

Observe how your breath changes with each activity and especially with each emotional state. When stressed out, you may experience shortness of breath, when tired or depressed your breathing will consist of mainly exhalations. When you are falling in love your breath will be fast or suddenly be "taken away" for a moment. Your emotions control your breathing. Therefore when you learn to control your breathing you will be able to control your emotions. You are the one in charge. Listen to your breath carefully. Are you mainly an inhaler? Do you tend to inhale strongly but rarely exhale deeply? If so, then you are by nature hectic, restless, anxiety ridden and find it hard to slow down. You need to learn how to deeply exhale. Make an effort and practice deep and slow exhalation and notice immediately how quickly you can enter a relaxed state. Are you a natural exhaler? Do you mostly exhale and rarely take a deep courageous breath? If so, chances are you're always tired, sluggish, pessimistic and not too open to new adventures. For you, it is time to learn how to inhale and welcome the life energy into your body and revitalize your every cell of it. Regardless of your breathing habit, here is a simple exercise that will help you achieve and enjoy deep, relaxed and calm state of your entire being. You need only a few minutes of practice to enjoy long lasting benefits.

YOUR INNER CONVERSATION

"I am taking a few minutes for myself. I need and deserve this time.
I can remember how to breathe correctly. I will be patient with my body.
With each inhalation I welcome the fresh new life energy and with each
exhalation I release any tension that I carry. I am relaxed and know that I can
experience deep inner peace within minutes of mindful breathing each day.
I am creating a new positive and healthy habit for myself".

EXERCISE

Sit comfortably. Place both feet equally on the ground. Make sure that your back
is nice and straight, so that you may breathe into every part of your being. Now
take your hands and place them with palms turned inwards on your solar plexus/
stomach area. Breathe through your nose only. Inhale and feel the stomach and
solar plexus area relaxing and expanding, while the shoulders stay down, nice
and relaxed. Only your lower chest and stomach are expanding, everything else
remains still, like a beautiful sculpture. Really relax the stomach muscles and let
all the tight, toxic energy out of that area. You will only achieve that if you really
physically loosen up and expand your stomach with each inhalation.
When you exhale, pull your stomach area lightly inwards, contracting the
stomach muscles. Repeat this easy, slow breathing exercise and with each
inhalation expand your stomach and gently contract it when exhaling. Notice how
energy is starting to circulate in your entire body. Energy that may have been
kept deep inside your solar plexus area will now surface and a sigh of relief will
overcome your being. Let out a sigh if you wish, just let go and completely relax.
An easy way to time your breathing is to inhale slowly and count to five honest
counts. Now hold the breath for five equal counts, and then exhale the breath for
five counts and lastly hold the exhalation for five more counts. Repeat for a few
minutes. Notice how calm, peaceful and serene your entire body is quickly
becoming. You may feel like yawning, which is your body's natural way of
releasing deep stress and pent up energy. After a few minutes, remain still and
enjoy the state of profound peace that this simple exercise will provide.

AFFIRMATION

Add a mental affirmation to your practice and repeat with each breath:

**"I exhale all excess negative emotions and with each breath
I welcome new and positive energy, ideas and people into my life."**

Repeat this exercise any time during the day, especially first thing in the morning
upon awakening and before you close your eyes at night.

JOURNAL

Mark in your journal the date when you first started this breathing exercise. Observe your habit and way of breathing. Do you tend to focus on inhaling or exhaling? Strive to balance the two and enjoy the state of deep relaxation you can achieve. Think of particular situation or person in your life that present most challenge for you at this time. Again note how your breath changes, just by thinking of them. Concentrate, breathe and focus on exhaling the stress level that someone or something may cause you.

Before going to bed at night, note your daily events and what emotions you experienced in connection with them.

Breathe and release the excess energy that these events still requite of you. Each day write down your emotional state and observe how quickly proper breathing helps you release stress and experience inner peace. You will be amazed at the rapid progress of your newly acquired healing breath technique and the profound effects of it on your entire life.

10. TALK and LISTEN to YOUR BODY

It is essential for your health and well being to develop healing communication with your body. Some of us are more "in tune" with our bodies than others. Body attunement is a very important part in your process of achieving inner peace. Knowing, feeling and hearing your body's messages is something that can be easily acquired.

Your body is an amazing and sensitive creation. It has an astonishing self healing and communication capacity. When you learn to concentrate and listen to its messages, it becomes a great self healing asset to you.

It is important that you realize this does not mean that you panic every time you feel a discomfort or you obsessively look for ailments.

It means fine tuning your mind and connecting it with your body.

By practicing this technique, you are on your way to becoming one in your body, mind and spirit.

YOUR INNER CONVERSATION
Visualize your body and begin the inner dialogue:
"Hello. How are you feeling today?
Is there anything in my body that requires my attention?
Am I holding unnecessary energy somewhere in my body that I need to release?
I will intuitively and energetically look through every part of you and listen for any messages waiting to be heard and noticed."

EXERCISE
You may practice this exercise while sitting or lying down.
Make yourself comfortable and relax.
Close your eyes. Focus the mind on your body. See yourself from head to toe. Now you are ready to begin.
Inhale thru your nose while expanding your solar plexus and stomach area and exhale by relaxing and slightly pulling your stomach in.
Continue this way of breathing throughout the entire exercise.
Let's scan your body. Concentrate deeply and focus on your feet. In your mind see the toes, the heels and whole foot. Inhale and visualize filling your feet up with while healing light. Exhale and completely relax. Continue to your ankles. Move onto the calves, knees, thighs, and hips. When you're done with each section, fill it with white healing and protective light.
Continue upward to the reproductive organs, lower abdomen and stomach. Each time you move into the next part of your body, take a deep calm and long breath. When you're done with the mental scan, fill the area with healing white light. Move higher to the solar plexus, always inhaling and exhaling deeply. Let

the air come into your lungs, heart, chest and shoulders. Again fill them with white healing light. Scan you entire lower back, mid back area and upper back. If you are feeling tension or discomfort in any particular area of the body, stay there for a few moments and breathe deeply into it. Try to put the discomfort and pain into a shape of a small gray cloud. See it and hold it with your mind. Now inhale deeply and when you exhale, visualize the gray cloud leaving your body. Repeat the visualization with each exhalation. Continue until the entire gray cloud is completely gone. Now replace the area where there was discomfort with bright white healing light. Concentrate firmly on exhaling your tension and replacing it with healing light and peace.

Continue with the visualization thru your fingertips, hands, lower and upper part of the arms and shoulders and your neck area. Inhale into your face, chin, cheeks, mouth and lips. Now continue to your nose, eyes, ears and forehead. Take your time for each area and concentrate with deep inhalation on each particular part of your body. Breathe into the back of your head and the top of your head. Every time you feel a discomfort, breathe deeply and exhale visualizing the small gray cloud leaving you body. Replace it with brilliant white healing light. Breathe in the white light and embrace the feeling of peace and love.

INNER CONVERSATION
As you enjoy the stillness and visualize your body, conclude with communication:
"I have looked everywhere and I recognized your messages. I am glad you reminded me of areas that need my help. I am always paying attention to you, listening and want you to be healthy. You are appreciated, heard and loved."

NOTE
If there is a particular area where you repeatedly feel pain and discomfort try and alleviate it with breathing into it and visualize a white light. In case of persistent pain or discomfort always consult a physician and seek medical attention. Visualizing white healing light when dealing with disease is beneficial and will not harm you in any way. With regular practice you will learn to perform this exercise faster and in any environment. This is a very good way to stay centered and in touch with your body's physical health. It is your way to communicate with your physical self.

AFFIRMATION

Repeat any portion or in whole this affirmation throughout the exercise.
**"I am sending love and healing light to every and each cell of my body.
What I do not need, I release. I am in charge of energies permeating my
being and physical body. I am filled with bright white light that heals,
energizes and protects me..."**

JOURNAL

Note in your journal any discomforts that you experienced in any particular area
of your body. Note the date and do not disregard any personal emotional
experiences connected to that particular time. It will serve as a great tool when
you learn to understand your body's messages on a deeper level.

It is also helpful to pay attention to which area of your physical body seems to be
most challenged by your energy distress. Connect the emotional meaning with
the corresponding chakra field. For example, if you experience persistent and
continuous discomfort in the stomach area, examine your feelings of anger, fear
or hatred that you may harbor. Remember how integrated our beings are with
every source of energy. This will become most beneficial and useful on your
journey of self discovery and help you achieve a state of true inner peace.

11. RELIEVE STRESS

When the vibration of our environment becomes filled with unharmonious energy, we experience stress. Stress is unhealthy. Ad one of the leading health problems of our times it creeps into everyone's life at one point. Whether we are at fault or we allow a set of circumstances to get the best of us, stress appears instantly and is a slow visitor to depart. However, becoming aware of the stress source and limiting our time in an unharmonious environment or relationship can eliminate stress and greatly improve our life. Stress can become a thing of our past, if we truly and honestly do something about it. The other option is to ignore it and let it take over your life. After a while, your body will give in and an illness will force you to slow down and pay attention to the stress level you have absorbed.

When you are in perfect health, your body vibrates at a harmonious level. Any outside stress factors disturb that perfect harmony and cause an imbalance. Disharmony affects your entire body - all your cells. The center of imbalance may concentrate in the area energetically and emotionally most connected to the stress. To help you understand your body's energy structure, it is important to be familiar with the energy centers - chakras listed in the introductory chapter of this book. This basic knowledge will become very helpful when you are ready to look at your unresolved stressful emotions and recognize how they affect your everyday emotional and physical state. For example: emotions of fear will concentrate in your stomach and affect your digestion, difficult heart and love situations may affect your chest area, heart, breathing and lungs.

The unharmonious vibration will affect your entire body like a domino effect, but first it will concentrate in that specific energy center that it corresponds with and is connected to your emotional core of the problem. You may start feeling unwell, or not at ease. That is the preliminary state of dis-ease.

Addressing and eliminating stress from your life is therefore of great importance. By ignoring it, it will only catch up with you sooner or later.

Relieving stress on a regular basis will become your best and healthiest habit. It will help you protect and preserve your health. Regular practice of relaxation and de-stressing exercises will help you attract peaceful people and circumstances into your every day life.

INNER CONVERSATION
In preparation for this exercise, find still your mind and repeat:
"I will give myself the present of this relaxation journey to protect my health
and maintain my strength, inner wisdom, and peace on all levels.
The wild waters of life will run by me, and I will remain unscathed and ever calm.
My peace will affect others and magnify the healing vibration around me."

EXERCISE

Find a calm and peaceful place. Sit or lie down and relax completely. Practice your deep long healing breathing. As you relax deeper and deeper, listen to your breath. In your mind and with ease lift yourself gently from your body and see yourself below. Now adjust your inner vision and notice your energy centers – chakras of your body.

FIRST CHAKRA is situated at the base of your spine. This chakra corresponds with your feelings about survival, financial security, vitality and foundation. How do you feel about your life in these areas? Acknowledge truthfully any anxiety you may be holding, concentrate deeply breathe and exhale any emotional pressure.

> **"I am exhaling all stress and I feel secure,**
> **vital and connected to the unlimited source of Earth power."**

SECOND CHAKRA is located in the area of sex organs. This chakra is connected to your sexual expression, creativity, procreation and family. Relax and ask yourself how you feel about your life regarding these emotions? Answer honestly and concentrate and deeply breathe and exhale any emotional pressure.

> **"I am exhaling stress and I feel sexually empowered,**
> **creative and grounded in my family life."**

THIRD CHAKRA is located at the area of solar plexus. This chakra corresponds to your ego, intellect, the mind and is a strong emotional center. Feelings of anger and fear tend to gather in this center. Relax and ask yourself if you hold any of these unresolved emotions in that area of your body. Answer honestly, concentrate deeply, breathe and exhale all stress and anxiety associated with these feelings.

> **"I am exhaling all stress and feel safe, at peace and secure in who I am."**

FOURTH CHAKRA is located in the area of the heart This chakra corresponds to all matters of the heart, love, self love, compassion and faith. Relax again and acknowledge the state of your love and heart matters. Concentrate on the feelings you find, breathe and deeply exhale all tension.

> **"I am exhaling all stress and feel loved and cherished by the divine power."**

FIFTH CHAKRA is located at the area of the throat. This chakra represents all matters of communication, truth, higher knowledge and your voice. Relax and ask yourself how strong you feel in this area of your life. Do you know how to speak your mind and voice your true self? Acknowledge truthfully your inner most answer, breathe and deeply exhale any tension and stress.

"I am exhaling all stress and feel secure in voicing who I am,
what I do not want in my life and what I need to be happy."

SIXTH CHAKRA is located in the area of the Third eye. This chakra is your connection to intuition, inner vision and the Third eye. Concentrate deeply on that area and your higher self, and ask how connected you feel to your inner voice? Relax, breathe, and wait for the answer. Exhale any doubts and stress.
"I am exhaling all stress and open up my inner eye into infinity to absorb
and make use of the knowledge and guidance available to me at all times."

SEVENTH CHAKRA is located at the top of the head. This chakra is your connection to the universal God consciousness and the heavens. Ask yourself honestly how often do you pay attention to this divine universal creative power. Patiently await the answer, breathe and exhale all negative feelings and anxiety.
"I am exhaling all stress and I trust the divine power that protects, guides
and loves me in any circumstance and without judgment, now and forever."

JOURNAL

Note in jour journal what feelings you discovered for each particular chakra. Follow up with regular practice and observe how life's circumstances affect you and your stress level. Make every effort to eliminate the stressful circumstances and nurture peace in your everyday life. Note all positive changes you experience after regular practice of this exercise.

12. RECHARGE IN STILLNESS

Every day life circumstances and challenges drain our energy. Sometimes just getting up and starting your day seems like a major effort. Many of us suffer from chronic fatigue syndrome or another exhaustion related condition. Scheduling time for relaxation is never on our agenda and if so, do we really come around to it? Often a serious disease or accident forces us to finally slow down, and pay attention to what our body was desperately trying to tell us.

Why did we have to wait so long to pay attention to something as important as rest and peace in our life?

You are in charge, and no matter how crazy your schedule and obligations may seem, you must take responsibility for allowing your burned-out state to escalate to this level.

Certainly we all need to work in order to gain our daily bread, but if we get into habit of being a workaholic, our health will suffer and some day we will have to pay back for all the times we refused to simply be still, breathe and let be.

Life without stillness is a never-ending race.

Are you aware that it will really make a tremendous difference if you shorten your busy schedule for a half an hour and schedule a relaxation time for YOU?

Honest desire to bring peace into your life needs an honest effort to achieve just that.

It is helpful if you look at relaxation this way: it is as important and meaningful as anything else on your daily schedule, as a matter of fact, even more. No one to impress, no one to justify, or explain to. This is you and your recharging time.

Do you let others tell you when you can go to sleep? I hope not.

Likewise, give yourself permission to take care of yourself and your health.

Many of you will notice how much better and stronger your creativity and productivity will become in return. Every engine needs a rest sometime and so does your human engine…your body.

Fill your body's energy battery in a few moments of complete stillness every day and become an indestructible being of power.

EXERCISE

This exercise can become your daily routine. Schedule it into your daily plan so that your body will know there will be a designated time for recharging and rest. In the beginning observe your body's rhythm. At what point during the day do you feel most energy depleted? If at all possible, that is when your body most needs some stillness. If your obligations are such that you must wait till the day is over, schedule at least a ten minute break as soon as you can. Your family must learn to respect your need for rest and all else can wait for those ten minutes that you need. If you are firm in your schedule, you may start a new and positive habit for your whole family. They may adjust to you and hold peace during your time of stillness. All else can wait, and since ten minutes is a really reasonable time for a complete break, make your best effort to implement this new habit.

A peaceful environment is essential for this exercise. You may want to use some soothing music to create a relaxing atmosphere. Create a short daily ritual. Have a cup of tea, sit or lie down and breathe. All else can wait. Breathe long, deep and slow and completely relax your body. With each breath you sink deeper and deeper into a complete state of relaxation and stillness. With your mind lift yourself from your body and float up towards the ceiling of the room.

Look down below your spirit self and see your physical body resting. You are deeply relaxed. With ease and lightness elevate yourself up and thru the ceiling of the building. Now you are above the roof of the house. Look around and notice other houses and the immediate environment where you are. Notice the gardens, the city or whatever area your home is in. You can see all of it below you, becoming more and more distant. Lift yourself even higher and higher out of your town, higher and higher up towards the clouds. You are floating lightly and with ease, becoming lighter and lighter and flying further and further from the Earth's surface. Look below and see how far the ground is. You are enjoying this journey and feel happy and care free. As you fly higher you finally reach the clouds. There is an especially beautiful, sparkling, light and very comfortable small cloud waiting just for you. Descend on that cloud with ease. A large and comfortable cloud-like lounge chair awaits you. Sit down and make yourself very comfortable. You feel warm and safe. Look around and see other clouds floating around you changing shapes and disappearing into the atmosphere. Your cloud is traveling and carrying you wherever you desire. Look down from the cloud and far into the distance below. You are far away from all the troubles and worries of your daily life and nothing else matter right now. Just breathe, relax and enjoy your floating cloud. Now your cloud gently lifts up and brings you onto a new higher level of atmosphere. Notice the beautiful sun above the clouds. It shines on your gently with a golden light. Every ray that touches your body vibrates with tremendous life force energy. Your body soaks up all this golden light and feels instantly energized, refreshed and recharged. With each breath you inhale the golden rays of power, and feel yourself becoming stronger. Breathe in the sun's light until you feel your body completely permeated with this golden sun power. When you feel ready, tell the cloud to gently bring you lower to the ground. Your cloud floats and descends lower and soon you see below the city, the buildings and the roof of the house where you are. Descend off the cloud and with ease descend lower thru the roof of the house, and lower until you find yourself just under the ceiling of the room. See your body below you, relaxed rested and filed with golden sun power. Happily descend into your body, deeply inhale and exhale and join your physical self. You are feeling refreshed, energized and happy. Now you are ready for the rest of the day.

AFFIRMATION
**"I am filled with the golden energy of the Sun.
The all powerful, everlasting fire that vibrates in every cell of my body magnifies my power and protects my health."**

JOURNAL
Note your personal time of the day when you suffer most from exhaustion. Create a time slot in your daily schedule for this exercise and keep notice of different times you felt you needed this exercise the most, what preceded this state and how the exercise affected your energy level afterwards.

Keep records of what activities, situations, environments or people seem to drain your energy level. This will provide a great guideline for changing your patterns and preventing needles energy waste and exhaustion.

Also note what situations energize you and help you maintain and magnify your individual power.

13. GOOD NIGHT'S SLEEP

One of the problems we may experience at some point in our lives is restless nights and lack of much needed sleep.

Many things occur during your sleep. Your body relaxes and replenishes for another day of activity. Your mind travels on a journey and may live thru adventurous and enlightening dreams and receive dream messages.

Your breathing pattern changes and you loose the sense of time.

To enjoy this special time meant for your rejuvenation and rest, one must have peace in body, mind and spirit.

For a peaceful and calmer body, it is helpful to follow some basic guidelines. Your diet plays a large role. For a healthier and more restful sleep do not consume a late, large or heavy dinner. Try to have an early meal.

If you do have a late dinner, avoid meat, very hot spicy foods and eat light.

Your sleeping environment is very important. It is not healthy to let yourself fall asleep in front of a television set, only to be awakened hours later by a disturbing sound. Computers and cellphones need to be turned off and out of bedroom.

Your bedroom is a place of rest and tranquility. Best colors to surround yourself with are pale blues, violets, whites with some pastel highlights and light pinks. Do not place wild blooming flowers at your bedside, as the aromas may evoke a different effect than sleep. Let some fresh air into your bedroom every day and keep the temperature a bit lower than the rest of your home.

A hot bedroom is not very comfortable and may lead to waking up feeling dehydrated and uncomfortable.

A cup of calming decaffeinated tea before sleep will help you prepare for rest. Respect and hear your body when you are feeling the need to retire for the night. Give yourself sufficient time to tend to your hygiene and get the much needed amount of sleep that you require. We are all different and as some of us need less or more rest, but on the average we need about eight hours of sleep a day.

Pay attention to what sensory energy you absorb, right before roaming off to bed. If you watch violent programming, chances are your dreams will be affected. Do what you can to always end your day in harmony with your dear ones. It is much more unproductive to let an unresolved disagreement hover over you all night as opposed to reaching some kind of harmony before sleep-time. Use the techniques in this book to induce a peaceful and calm state of mind. Do not analyze the daily scenarios back and forth, as you'll be tossing and turning all night. If you are not one of those lucky people who instantly falls asleep once you lay your head on the pillow, use this exercise so that you too may enjoy deeply rejuvenating and refreshing power sleep.

YOUR INNER CONVERSATION

"I am listening to my body and paying attention to its need for rest. I can feel it is looking forward to a deep and wonderfully rejuvenating and restful sleep. I am relaxing every part of my body. I am at peace with today, I did my best and now I deserve my rest. I will start tomorrow with a smile and have a new great day. I release all busy thoughts and dialogue from my mind and give my body a much-needed restful time for wonderful sleep."

EXERCISE

Lie down in bed and get comfortable. Close your eyes and slowly inhale and exhale deeply. Let out a sigh if you feel like it. Let yourself yawn. Lift your arms above your head and stretch your body. Make yourself comfortable, relax and breathe.

Visualize yourself sitting on the edge of an immense ocean. Observe the beautiful blue and turquoise colors of the ocean and the pale blue sky. It is a perfectly glorious sight. Listen to the sound of your breathing. Look far into the distance of the ocean and notice how each time you exhale a wave is coming gently towards you. Each time you inhale the wave retrieves back to the ocean. Watch this game and listen to the sound of it. You are one with the ocean; your breath and its waves are in perfect harmony. The ocean waves are in no hurry. They dance their perfectly designed rhythmical dance. It sounds like a soothing and relaxing lullaby. With each breath and each wave, you relax deeper and deeper. Your body is getting more and more relaxed. The sound of the ocean waves becomes distant. Now you are asleep at the edge of the ocean. The soothing sound of the ocean waves and your breath has put you into a deep and blissful sleep.

If you feel your mind wondering and wanting to analyze and rehash the events of your past day, worries or problems, simply focus your attention on the breath and the ever powerful ocean waves.

Your breath and the waves are one.

The power to move the ocean is in your breath.

AFFIRMATION

**"I am falling into a deeply relaxing, soothing, healing and blissful sleep.
I will awaken happy, holy and healthy."**

JOURNAL

Note your sleeping habits. How many hours of sleep do you need and how many do you get? Do you ever feel really rested in the morning or could you sleep for days? Sometimes you will require a few days of complete scheduled relaxation, maybe over a weekend where you allow yourself to catch up on all the lost sleep and start fresh. Make space in your day for this important rest.

Do you tend to ignore your body's signals when it needs rest and keep pushing yourself to extend the day?

Make an experiment and retire as soon as you feel sleepy in the evening. Observe how that affects you next day's energy level.

Do you wake up earlier than usual?

Do you feel more rested?

Does that affect your entire day's mood and energy level?

When you use this exercise, remember to be patient since you are creating a new good and healthy habit for yourself. Just as you have programmed yourself in the past to sleep less, now you are re-training yourself to relax and sleep when you need to. When you improve the quality of your sleep, it is most likely you will require less sleep than you thought.

PART THREE

Peace in Your MIND

14. RELEASE NEGATIVITY & ANXIETY

The key to releasing anxiety is in your mind. Why? Because most of the anxiety is created in your mind. Whether it is your past, present or future, worry and anxiety seems to be caused by your restless state of mind.

Becoming the master of your thoughts will give you powers on every level of your life. You are the one who decides what and when something is on your mind. Your wishes and desires are created and visualized in your mind first, so it is there that you can practice making your dreams a reality. How could you possibly get what you long for, if you cannot even imagine and visualize it in your mind? It is like a sportsman before breaking a world record. He sees himself achieving his goal and executing his routine in perfection. He must see it in his mind first. By being in charge of your mind, you can guide your life into any direction that you desire, and reach for your goals easily. Some of us feel that we can't help it, when nervousness, stress and anxiety attack our thoughts like a hidden enemy. We become restless with poor concentration, cannot enjoy life's moments of happiness, and get lost in anxiety and worry.

Your mind is very receptive and sensitive to outside stimuli. Your environment, sound, smell, color, touch, all living creatures and certainly other people - all of it affects your mind. Any vibration of the senses sends a signal to your mind that translates these messages for you. But you can also find yourself in a perfectly serene and quiet place and your mind is still wondering and racing out of control. One of the essential qualities for peace of mind is being able to release anxiety that you hold and learn to enjoy the present moment. Usually anxiety has little to do with the present. It revolves around something in the past or the possible future. Thus we have a tendency to completely miss out on the crucial time in life - the now. You can not change what happened and repeating in your mind your past actions is not very peace inducing. On the other hand, anxiety over the future will not improve it either. If anything, you will attract tension and disharmony. Therefore it is empowering to learn from past mistakes and let go, and visualize and affirm a positive future.

By enjoying the present we are positively affecting the future.

When you master your mind into the state of complete stillness and self control so no outside circumstance will disturb you, you will affect others in a similar way. They will wonder what is your secret and just being in your calm presence will affect them positively.

INNER CONVERSATION

"I am in charge of my thoughts. I decide what enters my mind and what I visualize. If negative, anxious thoughts enter my mind, I will simply release them and not give them any of my precious time or energy."

EXERCISE

Sit still and close your eyes. Concentrate on your breath, practice long and deep breathing. With each breath you are entering into a state of deeper relaxation. Now direct your concentration towards your third eye - your window to infinity. Unveil any foggy cloudy thoughts and create a crystal clear picture of a beautiful serene emerald green lake. The water is very still.

On the lake's surface are tiny curly waves from a light breeze.

The waves are barely there, moving in perfect harmony and order.

Someone comes by the lake. He throws a stone into the lake and suddenly the entire wave pattern changes. The perfect harmonious design pattern is gone, as the lake responds to the intruder by forming a circle of larger round waves around the point of stone's entry. Inhale deeply and exhale. With your mind calm the waves on the lake. Now the disturbance to lake's surface is gone, vanished. And the lake is back to its tiny and peaceful waves that dance with the breeze. Another person walks by the lake...he throws another stone into the water. With your mind concentrate and see the disturbing waves calm faster that the first time. Within moments the lake surface is back to the peaceful harmony.

Use the power of your mind and see the picture of the water's surface quickly calming down.

Beautiful large pine trees surround the lake. Suddenly the wind is blowing with great force and the trees are barely resisting the strong force. Concentrate and with your mind visualize the trees standing strong and firm. The wind does not affect them. Visualize slowing down the wind with the power of your mind.

Now visualize yourself waking up in the morning. Notice the first anxiety ridden thought that enters your mind. Now concentrate, breathe and with the power of your mind calm your thoughts and remain calm and centered.

Breathe and regain the power of your mind. Create a picture of peace and serenity and visualize yourself so. This visualization exercise will help you control, calm and center your mind. Exhale and release any tension that you may carry within your mind and replace it with peace.

AFFIRMATION

**"My mind is powerful and I am in charge.
I can calm any wave of my restless mind and release any stress or anxiety.
I can create and sustain harmony and inner peace."**

JOURNAL

Make note of the thoughts that make you restless.

Practice this exercise and consciously make an effort to eliminate the anxiety associated with various circumstances.

Each time you consciously use your mind, you are reminded of its tremendous power. Controlling your mind is essential when you want to eliminate anxiety from your life.

Acknowledge and learn what and who causes you anxiety, and consciously eliminate interaction with them as much as possible.

Make note of situations that bring you peace of mind.

Make sure that you regularly experience the environment, situations or people that help you bring and establish peace into your life.

15. PEACE AT WORK

We all desire to have peace and harmony in our demanding work environment. The fact is, that with the power of your mind, you can most positively affect and transform your coworkers.

Many times I am asked the following question:

"I can create peace for myself in my work environment, but my coworker or boss is difficult and negative. How do I deal with a negative person in my immediate work environment?"

There are many answers. First, do your best to not let it affect you. When someone's behavior is upsetting you and you spend time and energy rehashing the situation you are also giving them your own energy. Many people thrive on sucking the "life" out of you, basically living off your energy. It is important to be aware of that and take precaution.

It is best to resolve the matter without conflict, but a confrontation may be necessary. A conversation with a smile, gentle voice and kind words will help evoke a more peaceful reaction. Attack triggers attack. A smile calls for anyone to smile back. When you are upset, it is much easier to scream in disharmony at the one that has upset you, than to smile and be kind. Establish peace with your disposition.

One must remember that everybody is human and compassion is a great quality. You need to heal the relation with this person with patience and focus. If you cannot avoid them, prepare for a peaceful, but firm and confident interaction. Know what your goal is. If you want harmony and need to voice your dissatisfaction, calmly state your intentions. You may want to affirm a positive quality of your relationship first (you may have to search deeply), in order to place the person on a receptive non-defensive level.

Then calmly state your concern, unhappiness and problem. Explain your needs. If personal conversation seems impossible, you may try to improve the situation energetically. I have tried the following exercise technique many times when all else seemed to have failed and have always experienced surprising and unexpected success in resolving the most challenging conflicts.

Experiment with this exercise and see for yourself.

Most of all, release any expectations. Let the results surprise you.

INNER CONVERSATION

"I realize I am facing a challenging situation, but am eager to learn from it.
I will now consciously project healing energy into this relationship, so that I may enjoy harmony, feel productive and appreciated in my working environment."

EXERCISE

Find a quiet place, sit or lie down and close your eyes.
Practice the healing deep, long breathing.
See yourself surrounded with bright white healing light. Visualize the light shinning all around you. Concentrate and expand the healing light.
Breathe into your brightness and feel it magnify.
Now visualize the person you wish to have harmony with. See him/her near you. Look in to his face and eyes. Notice the emotion in his eyes. Let your mind gather only the positive thoughts about him. Open your heart to compassion. Remember that his inner suffering is causing him to be hurtful to others.
He needs and longs for love. Maybe he never experienced it. You will teach him and let him experience love on a subconscious energetic level. It could be to frightening for him to be physically present while you shower him with love energy. He might be afraid of breaking down and exposing his vulnerability, pain and suffering. He is trying to be brave and put up a tough front. He is acting according to what he has seen, grown up with, and experienced. Now you will send him loving thoughts. Visualize him smiling at you. All the anger, fear and negativity have gone. Visualize his eyes twinkling with love. Consciously concentrate and send him a big wave of love from your heart.
Surround him with white healing light. The light is glowing and expanding.
Project love into his entire being and heart center. Now his field of white light has expanded so far, that it has connected with your white light field. You are both surrounded with an immensely powerful and glowing healing white light.
There is nothing but pure love and light between you.

AFFIRMATION
**"I am making a loving effort to heal the relation between ...... and myself.
I am sending pure energy of love and light into his/her heart.
I surround them with white healing light."**

JOURNAL

Note the situations and people in your work environment that cause you unrest and stress.

Consciously practice this exercise in the morning before encountering and facing the situation, during the workday, and in the evening.

Start with a few minutes of your practice three times a day.

The change may be quick and sudden or take a while. But as soon as you make a conscious effort to lovingly improve the energy flow between you, a change in a positive direction will most certainly occur.

Follow up and note any and all changes that have occurred. Do not dismiss them as coincidence. There is no such thing and your energy vibration can have a very healing effect on the situation and person you have directed it to.

Follow the practice and see for yourself.

16. MIND PROJECTION

We have all experienced and heard those little negative and insecure voices that talk in our mind. A simple negative mind projection before you give yourself a fair chance can and will affect the pending outcome.

How many times have you caught yourself putting something down before it ever had a chance to happen?

Sentences like:

" I am sure I won't be awarded…. nobody is going to fall in love with me….. everybody is always against me….I never have any luck…nothing good ever happens to me… I am not good enough for that…" etc., run through your mind like wild animals. These thoughts take over, when you are frightened and angry. They create an energy block preventing positive events from occurring.

These are negative affirmations that we carelessly let affect us.

Why do we do that? Are we afraid of success? Do we feel undeserving?

Maybe we heard those affirmations a long time ago and they seem to sit so deeply in our sub-consciousness that we are completely used to them.

We give them free reign with our thought projections.

 Awareness is the key element. Are you aware of your thoughts? Stop yourself in the middle of a situation and catch your thoughts. Are you giving up, before you had a chance? Are you making excuses and preparing for failure before you ever thought of success? Do you visualize yourself failing, being disappointed and not getting what you want? Are you preparing excuses for family and friends, why you failed? All that before the event ever occurred, before you ever had a proper try and go at it.

Was your inner dialogue more like this:"If I fail, I will go home and cry in my pillow, watch a movie and go to sleep…"?

Or did you give yourself a chance of succeeding with thoughts like:

"I will give it my best and strongest and accomplish my goal. I will succeed!"

There is a vast difference between these two outlooks.

And , once again your mind cannot be underestimated.

It guides, projects, directs and affects your life in every aspect.

Discovering your thought patters can be fascinating. Once you realize how much of your life goes according to your pre-decided and self–affirmed plan in your mind, you will be truly amazed. How many times have you heard a successful person state: "I always knew in mind that I will succeed, that I will achieve what I want…". It is the absolute unwavering certainly that successful people have in common. The certainty that they will succeed in achieving their dreams. You may call it self confidence, but it is definitely more than that. It is their mindset, and clear focus about the outcome of their future. They have do doubt visualized themselves in the successfully accomplished situation. They have seen themselves there, tasted it, and heard it. They knew that it is possible and within their reach. They have seen the happy family life that they created, touched the walls of the house they wanted, and tasted the success they desired. They have used the power of their mind to their advantage, to transform their dreams into reality. We all have that capacity. Every goal is as far or close, as you project it in your mind.

First, you must clear your mind of the negative, doubtful and unproductive voices that take up valuable mind-space and diminish your power.

How do you reclaim that power of your mind?

Pay attention to your thoughts. Is there ever anything positive that you hear in your mind, about you, your dreams and desires? If not, you must create it. Instead of dwelling on the negative and getting upset why you hear and project only negative affirmations, begin to ignore them. Replace them with louder, more powerful positive thoughts and affirmations of success.

INNER CONVERSATION

"I am concentrating on releasing old unnecessary information. I am clearing my mind of anger and fear that I might be carrying within my psyche, and opening new space for self confidence and peace. I will empower myself with loving and peaceful thoughts that will positively affect my thinking patterns and help me realize my dreams."

EXERCISE

Find a peaceful and calm place. Relax, close your eyes and breathe with a long, deep healing breath. With your eyes closed lightly, gently elevate your gaze as if you were looking somewhere far into the distance, slightly above the horizon.

Listen to your breath. Concentrate deeply on the area of your Third Eye.

Inhale deeply and exhale. If a negative thought comes into your mind, simply but firmly state: "Go away". Do not dwell on it or get discouraged by it.

Disregard it and give it as little meaning as possible. Your mind is powerful enough to consciously decide what you are visualizing and thinking.

Visualize the word ANGER - as if you would write it across your inner screen. See each letter of the word. Visualize lighting a match and burning the word away. It disappears instantly.

Visualize the word FEAR - as if you would write it across your inner screen. See each letter of the word. Visualize lighting a match and burning the word away. It disappears instantly.

Visualize the word LOVE. See each letter of the word. It is composed of beautiful rose flower petals. Repeat the word in your mind and if you wish, speak it out loud. Repeat for a few minutes. Take a deep breath and exhale. See the flower petals shower your face and body.

Visualize the word PEACE. It is composed of beautiful white flower petals.
See each letter of the word and say it out-loud.
Repeat it and let it sink deeply into your sub consciousness.
Breathe with this inner mantra for a few minutes. Now, take a deep breath and exhale. See the flower petals shower your face. You can choose any positive sentence and project it onto your inner screen.
Practice this exercise every day and regain the power of your mind.

AFFIRMATION
"I am the master of my mind. I decide what I think, visualize and bring into my reality. The power of my mind is mine."

JOURNAL
Regaining control of your mind can be done with practice.
Make note of any feelings of anger or fear you may harbor.
Write what and whom they are connected with.
Use the exercise to erase them out of your mind. Let them go.
Make a list of emotions, things, and people that you desire to have in your life.
Visualize them within this exercise and see them come into your life.
Make notes of what you visualized and the results you achieved.
Keep your mind deeply focused and make space for peace projection.
The possibilities for your future are endless.

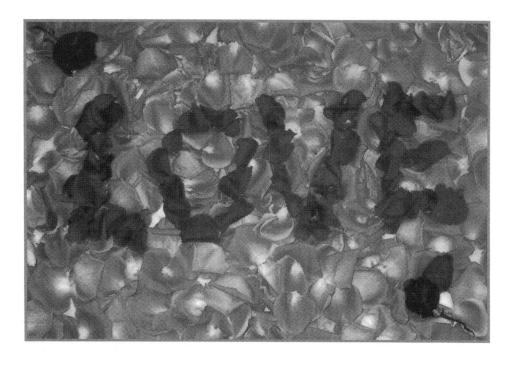

17. THE POWER OF POSITIVE AFFIRMATIONS

Your mind is an indescribably capable and powerful tool. It is essential for your inner peace to be aware of your mind's power. You are in control and you decide what occupies your mind. Just as you are in charge of how you nourish your physical body, you are also in charge of your mental nourishment. You allow images to affect it, music to transcend it and words to keep it occupied. Your mind is fast, it can jump from one topic to another and remember minute details. It has the habit of repeating scenarios over and over again like video footage.
It also keeps a lot of old data. Every sentence and event that happened to you is stored somewhere deep in your memory. The positive and encouraging affirmations you heard from your childhood until today, have helped you pursue your dreams and ambitions. Whenever someone believed in you and told you so, you engraved their energy into your positive memory bank. When you need to, you can revisit and replay those experiences in your mind.
But there are also negative and unpleasant sentences filled with self doubt that you allowed to stay with you. You may not necessarily need them, but refused or forgot to let go of them. Your old data is kept in your memory-mind archives. Often you can replay scene by scene in your mind. When your mind gets bored with the problems of the present, it digs into the archives and pulls something ridiculously dusty out for your review. It plays it in your mind to prevent you from hearing something new. You see, when your archives are filled up, there is no space for new, happy and positive data.
But the negative archives seem to always make space for more data.
You can and must create new space for your positive current and future events. Your mind doesn't necessarily like that. It is comfortable with the habit of playing old familiar tunes. It is essential to keep your mind flexible, ever ready and open to new possibilities.
The power of positive affirmations transcend all negative energy frictions you experienced. Have you observed a sportsman's concentration before a jump? Do you think there is any space for self doubt in his mind before he breaks the world record? Absolutely not! He sees himself successfully completing his performance. His mind is set. The positive affirmation in his mind is essential for his success. Same goes for everyone else from doctors, performers, teachers, artists, cooks. Everybody and anybody needs to hold a positive affirmation and vision in their mind in order to successfully complete a task. Do you think a flower designer has a negative affirmation when he is creating a bouquet? He knows what he wants and knows it will look exactly the way he envisions it- beautiful.
A doctor has to be positive about a surgery and mindful of every surgical move he performs on a patient. A teacher has to be confident about standing in front of his class to come across as a source of knowledge.

You need that positive voice in your mind that helps you successfully achieve anything you desire. If you allow a negative fear based thought to enter your mind, you will attract what you fear most. Consciously place positive self assured thoughts in your mind and proceed on your way. Anything is possible and can be done. Believe!

INNER CONVERSATION

"I am aware of the power of my thoughts. I will consciously concentrate on disregarding the weak voices of negativity that may want to penetrate my mind and am going to find my positive power. I am affirming peace, happiness, love, health and success in my life now and always."

EXERCISE

Relax and concentrate on your breath. Listen to your mind. Listen to the actual words that travel in your head. Pay attention to the images that are projected in your mind. Now, still your mind and listen to your breath only.

Visualize your head. Look at the shape of your head from all sides. This is your command center. This is where memories and ideas reside. It is a big and busy office. There are many halls in this office-building, look and observe them.

You'll find he hall of your childhood, your fears, addictions, loves, good memories, laughter, tears, ambitions, disappointments and deep expectations, dreams and many more. There is a very specific hall that you are looking for. It is the hall of positive thoughts that helped you experience the best and happiest moments of your life. Look for it and find it. It is big hall. Above the door hangs a large sign that says:" Yes, I can…All dreams are possible"

You enter this hall. There are a few stunningly beautiful armoires in the middle of this large hall. You open one and see it is filled with books that contain all your positive thoughts you ever thought of. Here are all different sentences that you've heard in your life from people you've known or met, people who love you and believe in you and have encouraged you to pursue your dreams.

They are also your thoughts of times when you achieved and realized your dreams. When great things happen to you, you are thinking in a positive way. When someone gives you a compliment, they are sending you positive energy. All those loving moments are stored in this hall and you can read the titles on the covers of these books:

"I am strong. I am lucky. I am rewarded. I can do it. I am falling in love. I feel beautiful. I am smart. Yes, I can. Great things are coming my way. I am protected. I am loved. Happiness is with me. I am healthy. Every dream can come through. I can work hard. I am disciplined. I am open minded. I am intuitive. Yes, I can! I am loved…. I am loved…"

Even if you don't remember when you heard and if you've heard this words in your life, they are there, they do exists. You are lucky, unique, beautiful in your own special way and very much loved.

You like this hall. In it is the key that helps your every dream come through... There are no negative messages in this hall. It is filled with love for you, your life, your family, friends and all living creatures of the universe. Look at every word in your books of positive and happy thoughts and in your mind, take them with you. Now you can leave the hall. Again, you see the office building that you visited. Now visualize yourself distancing away from it, relax and come back into your physical body. With you, you've brought back every happy and loving thought from your special place in your mind. You can visit your hall of "all dreams possible" anytime you need or want.

AFFIRMATION
"I realize the power of my mind. I think, allow, attract and choose positive and loving thoughts into my mind."

JOURNAL

Note all positive affirmations you have thought of in your past that helped you achieve and realize your dream. Small ones, big ones, it doesn't matter. It is important to know how powerful of an effect they've had on you. Now, note all things you would like to accomplish. Next to that, write a positive affirming sentence. Practice using these affirmations, saying them out loud and sending the energy message out into the universe. Visualize yourself accomplishing goals that you affirm. Note the positive results and different circumstances that help you realize your dreams.The universe adjusts and moves around our energies and frequencies.

Your mind is very receptive for receiving positive affirmations during these specific times: first moments of waking up, anytime you meditate, when physically exercising, before or after taking a nap and before falling asleep at night. Practice this fun an easy exercise anytime, especially at the above mentioned times and notice how your entire outlook on life and self confidence will improve.

18. YOUR HOME IS YOUR TEMPLE OF PEACE

The purpose of this chapter is to help you create a nurturing and peaceful home environment. Some say that the environment is stronger that the will.

If you place a person into an unharmonious environment, chances are he will be affected by it in a negative way. Similarly, if you place a negatively charged person into a harmonious environment, he will respond accordingly and with time reach a more positive, calmer state.

Many environments that you experience throughout the day cannot be changed. You pass thru them; sometimes feeling depleted, or unraveled by them. However, your home is different. The great advantage is that you can control and change your home to suit you better, adjust it to your desires and let it make a positive influence on your life.

Your home is your temple. It is the place where you sleep and gather your thoughts, dream your dreams and wake up to a new day, find another chance to embrace a new experience. You get nourished, let your guard down, and if you need to, safely release your anxiety and shed a few tears. Your home reflects your state of mind. If everything is disorganized and untidy, there is not a chance that you are very clear or orderly in your mind about anything.

Creating order in your home environment will help you find and develop concentration skills and clear your mind.

There are those, who go to the other extreme. Everything is obsessively clean and spotless. There is a sure chance that such a person is quite a perfectionist, critical of others and himself and rarely content with anything. Such a person may have an obsessive and restless mind as well.

The key is moderation and finding balance in every aspect of your life. Your environment has a great influence on your overall feelings and state of mind, so when you consciously create a comfortable, serene, loving and peaceful home environment, your home will become the nurturing temple that you need.

We all require some time by ourselves to clear the mind, soothe the body and listen to the voice of your spirit. No matter what size your home is, in it you can create these areas that will help you experience inner peace.

INNER CONVERSATION

"I love my home. I realize the importance of creating the vibration of harmony, happiness and peace in my home. I will make it my habit and pleasure
to explore, nurture and respect my personal temple.
Within it, I will rediscover myself, learn to grow, and master peace of mind
to carry with me wherever I may go."

THE BEDROOM

This is your sacred space for love, inspiration, rest and rejuvenation. To decorate use colors that soothe your soul and help you relax. Do not use this area for computer work, eating or entertaining. Confrontations and heavy discussions do not belong here. This is a place of peace. Cherish and guard it. Be selective as to who you let enter this area, as they will leave their energetic imprint.

AFFIRMATION: "This is my place of love, peace and beautiful dreams."

KITCHEN

This is the gathering area of your home. It is the place where you and your family and friends get nurtured on all levels. Have you noticed how many times at social gatherings everyone ends up in the kitchen? It seems that is where everything happens. Things are cooking in more ways than one.
Use lively, vibrant colors, and place fresh fruits on display. No matter how small your home, the kitchen is the nourishing center for your clan.

AFFIRMATION: "This is my place of healing nourishment."

OFFICE

No matter what your calling is, you must have a designated area where you can address your business, legal and personally creative space. Your thoughts in the abstract have great powers. When you put those thoughts on paper, they get another meaning; they seem to exist in reality. If you can write:" I love you…" to someone, it certainly takes on another level of reality, then if you just think it or even say it out loud. Therefore your office space is where you are putting your thoughts on paper and creating another level of reality. You can experiment by placing vibrant orange, red and yellow colors in this area.

AFFIRMATION: "This is my place for successful inner work and creativity."

LIVING ROOM - SOCIAL AREA

In this area your visitors get to experience your communication. They connect with your spirit. There is no place like home and when your closest friends get to join and share the comfortable environment that you have created, they experience a part of you that is special. Do not place all white black or dark colors here. Use a harmonious mixture and accent it with vibrant color touches. Flowers will liven up this area as well as great music.

AFFIRMATION:"This is my place for relaxed and enlightened conversation."

BATHROOM

This room is your personal spa destination. Before you begin your day, you need to feel rested, refreshed, and happy with your appearance. Make it a routine to pamper yourself and really enjoy some time alone. Take a bubble bath or long, soothing shower. Keeping this area organized will help you get ready quickly, so that you may find what you need, feel pampered, and see a complete physical image of yourself before entering the world. Splurge and give yourself that gift.

AFFIRMATION: "This is my place for rejuvenating beauty and loving care."

MEDITATION RELAXATION SPACE

Not everyone has the luxury of an entire room being dedicated to peace and meditation. But there is no need for that. You can choose a particular corner of your home that is your meditation sacred space. Create an altar with your favorite objects that have a special meaning to you. You will need a chair or sitting area for meditation, reflection, contemplation or visualization practice.

Let your other family members know this is your sacred space, that needs to be respected. A special corner in the bedroom or your office may be suitable for that. When you want to be with yourself and hear the voice of your soul, take refuge in this healing corner that you've created.

Remember that your vibration in that particular area will grow stronger with time and you will experience deep serenity and peace when visiting it. Create a ritual by lighting a candle, sipping tea or listening to soft music. This is your temple and your personal perfected environment for deep relaxation.

AFFIRMATION: "This is my sacred place of light."

JOURNAL

You won't be able to adjust your home overnight, but with time and care you can learn to enjoy the transformation of your home into a relaxing and peaceful place.

Make note of all areas that feel inharmonious or cluttered to you and adjust, eliminate and select the pieces of furniture. Choose your "personal reflection" corner and use it regularly.

Note how the changes in your environment at home have affected your overall feeling of inner peace.

Clear disturbing, negative energy with a sage bundle smudge stick. Always open all windows and doors and air out the room well. Repeat when needed.

PART FOUR

Peace in Your SOUL

19. YOUR INNER RELATIONSHIP

Discovering and understanding life starts with discovering yourself.

That seems to be the biggest puzzle. Why can we help friends, relatives, coworkers with fantastic advice, but when it comes to ourselves, we are clueless or far off?

Have you ever had an honest conversation with yourself?

Or was there never really any time or occasion for it?

Have you ever had a relationship with someone who never had any time for you and your thoughts, problems, worries, and never really wanted to hear what's on your mind? And if you did talk to them, it was very clear that they are just politely there, but not hearing you at all?

How would you feel in such a relationship? You wouldn't be happy, would you? Most likely you would feel neglected, lonely, forgotten and not very cared for or loved.

Many of us have a tendency to behave that way. With whom?

Well, sad but true, here is the answer: with ourselves.

When was the last time you sat yourself down and inquired about your deep happiness? About your dreams, desires and expectations?

You can have the best partner, job, career, family etc., but if you have no relationship to your spirit-self, chances are, you are not very happy or content with your life in general, despite the good fortune.

Making time for yourself and knowing how to listen takes special care and effort. You may not want to talk about yourself and your feelings too quickly.

You may want to avoid facing the deep truth and will make yourself unavailable for your interviewer...you.

Making yourself busy beyond belief without a moment to breathe often shows signs of soul self-neglect. You simply cannot face the truth, do not want to hear it or know it, so you run yourself into the ground from morning till late evening.

Then, you justify simply falling into bed and certainly not doing any inner reflecting or soul searching.

The day is over and so is the opportunity for your honest conversation.

But one day the inevitable will happen. You will become ill...hopefully only with a flu, cold, or at the most - a sprained ankle. Something will hit you to snap some sense into you - to make you stop, wait, and listen to your spirit and body.

You will have to be bedridden for a few days, hopefully run out of good programming on TV (that won't be hard), get of the web, and finally listen to your inner voice. Facing the inner most truth is difficult. Maybe you are in a situation you see no exit out of, and thinking about it would only make it worse.

Maybe you have no courage to go after your dreams, but want to play it safe, avoid facing reality and are basically making excuses for yourself and preparing for your self-predicted failure. There are many possibilities, but one thing remains clear and certain: in order to find any kind of inner peace, you must open the secret closets of your soul and face the skeletons in it. There might be noting frightening at all, just old dust, that is meaningless now, but by ignoring it you made it bigger than it is remembered. There is no better time than now, to face the ghosts of past and look into the eyes of the present. Then, you will see the clear road to the future. The relationship with your inner self reflects all your relationships. If you can't hear yourself - nobody else will neither. Now, let's listen.

EXERCISE

 Find a calm and peaceful place and relax. Breathe long deep and slow for a few moments and sense your body relaxing and slipping into a deep state of inner calm.

Visualize yourself on a beautiful deserted island. It is late afternoon and the sun is comfortably warm. There is nothing in sight for miles and all you see is beautiful ocean and a sandy beach. Smell the air and listen to the sounds around you. You are walking on the beach. Every step you take relaxes you deeper and deeper. Breathe and soak in the gentle sun and lovely environment.

Suddenly you notice a person far away, sitting under a tree.

You come nearer, but cannot see the person's face. They are turned away, wearing a big sunhat.

You don't know why, but something about this person fascinates you.

You have a deep need to know everything abut them.

You inquire if you can ask them a few questions? They answer, yes, but they do not have much time. You want to know everything about that person, but under the circumstances you will ask them only what seem to you the most meaningful questions.

You begin:

"What are you doing here? What are you looking for? Are you happy? Are you in love? Whom do you love? Who is the most precious person or thing to you? What brings you joy in life? What is your biggest desire? Do you have any major regrets? What is your dream? What is your biggest sorrow? What do you do for fun? Do you ever feel lonely? What are you afraid of? Who loves you? Is your life good? Where do you want to go? Do you have a best friend? Do you ever cry? "

You hear a gentle voice, and get shy but honest answers to all your questions. Just when you can not stand it anymore, and you want to know who this endearing, fascinating person is, they turn around.

It is YOU. You have just met your mirror image. And the answers you heard have been your answers. You rediscovered yourself and opened the door to your inner self.

AFFIRMATION
"I want to know myself. I want to listen to my inner voice and learn all there is to know about my deepest dreams, desires, sorrows and loves. I want to be my best friend."

JOURNAL
This exercise will teach you how to hold honest and clear conversation with yourself.

Note all the questions that you posed to your fascinating person on the beach and remember the answers. Where do you find similarities? Is there a deep desire somewhere to live in situations as that person described?

Do you recognize any of your trademarks, habits, and circumstances?

Pay attention and now ask yourself the same questions.

Observe the difference between answers of your imaginary friend on the beach and yourself. Maybe the friend was voicing your dreams and desires?

Repeat this exercise another time and notice the differences, now that you know who the mystery person is.

This exercise will help you greatly in beginning a conversation with your inner self and learn how to be aware, connected and balanced with your inner most desires, dreams and real situations that you are experiencing in your everyday life. Closing the gap between reality and dreams can only be done when you know the tiniest detail of both sides. Then you'll recognize that anything is possible.

20. PEACE WITH PAST AND YOUR FOUNDATION

Vibrations permeate every living creature in this world.

Music and sound, colors, aromas, people and events that we experience throughout our lives affect us with different vibrational frequencies.

Each one of us carries within our energy field information about our entire emotional past. The vibrations that surrounded and permeated you during a specific experience of your life stay within your every cell. Certainly your mother was experiencing different events and emotional stages when she was carrying you under her heart. Those vibrations embedded in you that particular energetic information. Your body is carrying all these various memory programs from your past. On a subconscious level you are aware of them and can recall them. To confirm certain information about the emotional state of your parents while they were expecting your arrival, you can ask your parents. What was their situation? A young couple expecting a child even under the best of circumstances feels a huge change approaching. Every little detail, like hesitation about commitment to each other, a rushed marriage, disharmony with in-laws, a big move, death in the family or a difficult older sibling have affected your being before your birth. You absorbed and stored the emotional information of your mother and father. You parents are very emotionally connected during the pregnancy. The mother is experiencing a tremendous change in her body and life, and remains energetically connected with your father even if he is absent. Feelings of remorse, fear or anger may torture her broken heart. Health issues like previous miscarriages may instill deep fear and anxiety in a new mother. Her emotional state will unquestionably affect her unborn child.

If you cannot ask your parents about the far distant past and events that surrounded your pre-birth and birth, you may explore therapeutic regression. Unveiling your past is most fascinating. Discovering the relationship between your parents and their parents while you were about to be born can be a wonderful journey towards your understanding and knowing yourself, and why you feel, act and think a certain way.

Once you were born, your life's journey began. Discovering the circumstances surrounding your actual birth will convey further information about your soul's energy adjustments upon arrival. Many times following a difficult birth or for health reasons, the child is taken away from mother and nursed by hospital personnel or relatives. Maybe you were deprived of much needed human loving touch within the first weeks of your life. Whatever the circumstances, your mission is knowing yourself, understanding as much as possible about what was your entrance and set-up for this life. You may be surprised and information that may seem meaningless to your parents, will create sudden revelations and a deeper inner understanding of yourself on a subtle level.

It will help you understand yourself and your predispositions, fears and anxieties or inner confidence and a sense of calm security.

A very important part of this journey is releasing any feelings of anger or resentment towards someone from your past, or even your parents. They did the best they could under their given circumstances, and it is in your best interest to forgive and let go. You are the one carrying excess unresolved emotions about them, so it is up to you, to make peace with your past. The present moment is what life is about and if you let your past rule the present, you are depriving yourself of the happiness that you could be enjoying now. Learn from the past and enjoy and relish in the present to create a happy and fulfilled future.

INNER CONVERSATION
"I will go on a journey of discovery about my descent into this physical body.
I will observe, listen and carefully note the memories that I call upon
and release and harmonize any unresolved, negative feelings I may carry.
I will cleanse my spirit and make room for uplifting and peaceful memories."

EXERCISE
You will need a notepad and a pencil. Find a calm peaceful place, sit down and relax. Breathe. Visualize yourself in a beautiful park. There is a bench not to far way and sitting on it are your young parents. They are in love, holding hands, smiling and looking into each other's eyes. Listen to them laughing and talking. Imagine the conversation and hear the tone of voices. Can you sense they way they feel? In love, in lust or just unaware of what is about to happen. Fast forward to a later day and time. You have been conceived and your mother just realized you are present. See her face, look into her eyes. Is she frightened, angry, or blissfully happy? Where does she go and whom does she tell first. Now visualize your father, as he is about to find out. Carefully observe his reaction. Is it filled with regret, anger, joy or ecstatic pride? Maybe he doesn't even realize what it all means. See yourself as a small energy ball in your mother's womb. How do you feel? Happy to be present, eager to experience life or hesitant and unsure?

Go to the next step and see your birth. Where are you? Who is there and what is the time? Is it night or a bright sunny day? Look at the room and see your mother. Any moment and here you are. What is your first deep emotional memory upon arrival? Take whatever far memory seems to float into your mind and be present in a very relaxed easy way. It is your birthday. You are here… where do they take you? If you are not with your mother, visualize and sense how do your parents feel about you not being with them …possessive, relief or worry? Whatever answer comes to mind, take it without analyzing and move on. Visualize yourself at 6 moths old. Who is with you? Are you doing well, healthy and content or a baby with crying fits and sleepless nights? Easy child for your parents or demanding and weary? All those details matter and will help you understand yourself and your emotional tendencies. They will infinitely expand your self-knowledge and magnify your understanding of yourself. Now see yourself ages one thru 7 and each time you see your young face, look into the eyes and sense how this child - YOU - feels. Loved, sad, unhappy or carefree, protected, nurtured, forgotten, mischievous and excited?

Every time you sense a memory thought floating by, write it down and continue with the pieces of the puzzle about yourself.

Continue this exercise until you come to age fourteen. Now rest and relax. You may read the notes you've written down and remember some more. Or you may want to distance yourself completely and continue in a few days. Be delicate and sensitive when it comes to calling upon your spirit and intuition to bring you back the memories of your past. There is certainly a difference between imagination and real memory. But within a state of deep relaxation, you can train your mind to stop all thoughts that don't belong there. It is a matter of relaxation and stilling the mind. Then your intuitive window to infinity will gladly open up for you and help you assemble the long lost, but so very necessary pieces of this puzzle.

AFFIRMATION
"My life is like a fascinating puzzle. I will take great care to find all the missing pieces and compose a perfectly clear picture so that I may understand and know myself."

JOURNAL
With time you will remember more and details may be revealed to you later that will help you make sense of the whole picture. Note every feeling and emotion that comes to you and without too much analyzing move on. When intuitive information comes to you, it is essential that you keep the concentration level undisturbed. Make separate notes for the information you received on your intuitive journey and the notes you add later. This will help you keep a clearer picture when you repeat the exercise and discover new and unexpected information.

21. FEARLESS LOVE

Falling in love is not planned. It happens one day when you least expect it. Love makes the world turn around, they often say. However you look at it, it is true that love is an essentially important emotion that influences your entire life. Happiness in love seems easily attainable for some and impossible for others. Most everyone has had an unhappy experience in love. Loving yourself is the key element for attracting positive experiences into your love life. The partner that we meet at the destined time will teach us new levels of emotional expansion and strength. Timing is always just perfect for your life's lesson. Learning from experience of the heart and seeing the deeper meaning for the evolution of your soul has an empowering effect. It is important to spend time in peace with yourself and listen to your heart. Are you truly happy and if not, what is holding you back? Do you know? Many times your everyday dissatisfaction is blamed on your partner, yet maybe he/ she has nothing to do with it. It is your own unresolved matters that are in the way of true happiness. The partner just seems to be there at the wrong place and the wrong time and basically anyone close to you would be " at fault " for your misery. But the truth is, it is in the depths of your soul where dissatisfaction, unhappiness and restlessness reside.

Feeling sorry for yourself, complaining and reanalyzing an old disappointment will not bring you any closer to a happy heart. Time for reflection and honest conversation with yourself is needed. A conversation with a friend may not do either, for you will conveniently change and adjust the facts so that you may get "off the hook" and avoid taking the responsibility for the situations you've created. What are your realistic expectations of your partner? Little daily disharmonies may suddenly take a meaningful aspect when you face the real facts. It is about you and your expectations. You and your mirror image that you need to face and live with. Maybe you'll complain the partner is never there for you. Are you there for you? Maybe he never listens. Do you listen to yourself? He is never attentive and kind. Are you to yourself? Very important questions. You may be Mother Theresa for everyone else, but to yourself, you wont give a kind word, a break, or a treat. How then do you expect others to magically guess what you need? You seem to need nothing. Silence and unspoken words may become heavier and unnecessarily powerful, if ignored for too long. Remember that compromise is present in every harmonious, loving relationship. Certainly sharing a life together is different than going trough life alone. But there are great things you can accomplish by being alone at times. If you want love in your heart and your life, a sacrifice must happen. There is now someone else to consider, their feelings, their needs and their preferences. Be kind to yourself and your chosen partner, communicate with your heart and learn to dance to the various tempos of the love dance.

INNER CONVERSATION
"I will visit my heart every day. I will listen and sing to it.
I will cherish it and trust its voice."

EXERCISE
Sit in a quiet place. Breathe long, deep and slow.

Visualize your heart energy center like a beautiful red rose. See its' petals and smell the scent. If your rose is a bud, open the bloom and enjoy its beauty. As you see this rose in your heart area, feel your heart opening wide and inhale deep, long and slow. Exhale and release any sadness or hurt you may be holding on to. Repeat and continue for a few minutes.

Remember the time when you were in love. Remember the person you were or are in love with. (You may also choose any person whom you love, for example: parent, child, friend..etc, anyone that you would like to permeate with love).

Visualize yourself in a bright sunny room with that person. They are standing in front of you, smiling at you with love in their heart. Open your heart and fully embrace the warm overpowering feeling of love that flows to and from your heart. Concentrate on that powerful feeling in your heart. Hear your breath and feel the amazing energy of love flowing thru your veins. Time does not exist, nothing else matters, just you and your love filled heart. Your entire being is glowing like a star.

Concentrate, breathe and expand the sensation of love, the exuberance of your entire spirit in a state of supreme bliss. Transcend this elated feeling and connect it with the joy of being alive. Every cell in your body is vibrating with this energy of love. Now direct your love energy to your Third Eye area, the window to infinity and the all-knowing spirit. Enjoy the calm, exuberant sensation of profound inner peace and love. Thus you have connected your heart and your mind with your higher self.

This blissful sensation of love is yours, available to you always, anyplace, anytime. You carry it within your heart wherever you go and share it with the rest of the world. When you meet a soul that recognizes and embraces your magnetic power, the love magnifies infinitely.

Love has the power to heal and manifest miracles. Approach a challenging situation by projecting this indestructible feeling of love that is available to you at all times. Bring yourself back to that feeling of love permeating your entire body and spirit. With this empowering self sustained love power, you can heal all your past love experiences, release any negative emotions and be prepared to welcome and sustain love in your life right now.

Unconditional love is fearless like a bird in the sky.

AFFIRMATION

"I carry within my heart an infinite power of love. It nurtures and empowers me. Every time I choose to awaken that power, it becomes stronger and more powerful. It heals all sorrows and makes way for new love."

JOURNAL

To begin with this exercise ask yourself a few honest questions and make notes:

Is your heart open?

Do you listen to your heart or do you have a tendency to analyze and rationalize everything in your mind?

Carefully reflect on your deepest desire for your love relationship.

Visualize how it manifests and works in your everyday life.

What are your expectations?

What you are willing to sacrifice for that?

What are you doing to make it possible?

Honest conversation with your heart will help you find the deeper reason for your possible unhappiness.

Repeat this exercise and answer the questions in a few days or weeks and see what changes have occurred.

How did your exercise influence your behavior in your love relationship?

Are you going in the direction that you desired and visualized?

Continue on your soul-searching journey and remember to listen to your heart's wishes so you can help make them come thru.

22. YOUR ACCOMPLISHMENTS

You are one of a kind. No matter how hard you try, you will never be like anyone else. And no one can be exactly like you. Thank God! Your destined life journey has as specially designated road that only you are privileged to travel on.

Your life's events and people you meet are especially chosen for your growing experiences. Your life journey really is a marvel. You came into this life with a special purpose. You have a mission. There are no small missions. Every detail, action, and intention counts and is important. Your efforts count. Your responses and your decisions matter. You are a perfectly fitting missing element in this world's puzzle that makes everything complete. Every sentence you say has repercussions. Small ones, bigger ones, positive, negative... it is a frequency that is yours alone, and it is floating in the universe now. It never disappears. It transforms but never evaporates into nothingness.

And even nothingness has a purpose.

Your life so far, has been like a carefully written film script full of unexpected twists and turns. If you were watching your life's movie, you would surely enjoy it. You would feel compassion, love and sympathy for the main character - you.

In your life and its circumstances you acted according to your choices. They were the best you were capable of, at that particular time. You did well.

And if you think you could have done better, think again.

Are you harder on yourself that you should be?

It's in the past and now here you are. It is your journey and only you know all the real, real tiny details that brought you here. You know all the secrets and hidden thoughts that played a role in the choices you made. And you did great.

Now you are ready for more. This very minute your life story continues further. Every minute holds the potential to change your life and bring new opportunities your way. How exciting!

It is important that you acknowledge resolution and contentment with your past and open the possibility for future exciting events. Your journey is ever new, fresh and full of possibilities. Your assignments change and expand.

It is never too late to recognize and realize your dreams.

INNER CONVERSATION

"I am ready to make peace with all my wonderful accomplishments big and small...I can see my life as an adventure and am excited about the future of my journey. My unique life travel has made me stronger, wiser, more compassionate and experienced. I can share this experience, help and advise, guide and protect those behind me. All that I've done matters and is seen by the ever watchful divine eyes. I love my life and look forward to new adventures coming my way."

EXERCISE

Relax and concentrate on your breath. Deep long exhalations and inhalations. Close your eyes. Be still and listen to your breath.

See yourself standing in a beautiful meadow. It is filled with wildflowers of all different colors. Take a walk and enjoy the marvelous colors all around you. Listen to the birds chirping and observe the butterflies resting on the blossoms. Now you meet a small child. They are planting and tending to wildflowers in the field, working hard and concentrating with all the power of their little mind. The flowers look lovely. Tell the child they are doing well.

Now walk a little farther. The meadow now becomes filled with small blooming bushes and shrubs. You meet a young adult. They are trimming some shrubs and clearing the way for your path. They are doing their best with their young hands but are not quite as experienced with the tools, as they would like. The youngster is working as hard as they can. Tell them they are doing wonderfully. Now, walk a little further. You find yourself amidst a beautiful, deep forest. There you notice a beautiful young person, all grown up.

They are working hard at clearing the big old trees that are blocking the forest path. The job is tedious, but they don't seem to shy away from hard wok and are determined to compete the task at hand. Thank and praise them for the hard work and tell them how important it is.

Now walk a bit further. Deep in the forest you find a small stream. A kind older person is sitting nearby, with wisdom written all over their ageless face. Their eyes are deep and all knowing. Their hands are holding magnificent wild berries, especially handpicked for you, and a wooden cup filled with fresh mountain spring water. They offer you this gift of the forest fruit and water. You thank them, eat the berries and drink the water, enjoying the deep rich flavor and tasting the freshness.

Your hunger and thirst are satisfied.

You are revitalized and ready to continue on your journey thru the forest.

Open your eyes. You are content with your past and at peace and confident about the path of your life's future.

The child, youngster, the adult and old wise person are images of your soul on your life's journey.

The berries are the fruits of your life's labor and the mountain water is your desire, forever running in your veins. You are but a traveler thru the forest.

Enjoy the journey, know you are on your way, awaited, taken care of, loved and nurtured, now and always.

AFFIRMATION
"I am here to fulfill my life's calling…I am blessed, confident and at peace that all is going according to a perfectly designed plan."

JOURNAL
Note your accomplishments in your life.
How do you feel about them?
Do you forget and ignore, or recognize your achievements?
Are you always self-critical?
Make peace with your accomplishments.
Return to your notes in a while and see how has this exercise influenced your feelings about your past accomplishments.

23. EXPAND YOUR WORLD

The limitations that we create for ourselves are there for a reason. Within them we have a space that we feel somehow in control of. The sheer concept of the endless possibilities can be overwhelming. Especially if we are not sure what we want. But one thing is certain, we all desire peace within our soul.
Everybody wishes they could influence and know about their future.
The truth is, we do have a say in our future. Our every word, thought and action vibrates around us and the cosmos acts accordingly. One action triggers another, a single word changes everything. "Hello" may not seem as meaningful as "I love you" but it can be. Had we not said "Hello" there would be no "I love you" eventually. Intertwined actions reflect our sensory perception and sensitivity. Limitations are there to be challenged and eliminated. It is very interesting to discover who sets up our limitations. Maybe a scolding sentence we heard as a child created a subconscious limitation. Someone's high expectation of us and the subsequent failure may have set up another firm limitation. Usually we have allowed others to set the limitations for us. It is important to remember that every successful person has failed many times before finally succeeding. But there was one crucial difference. For them, there were no limitations and if so, they strived to break them. There is of course also the question of character. Some of us may need a limitation in order to get motivated. When we get bored easily and want a challenge we create a situation that suits that scenario. Whatever we wish or desire for, we eventually get. Be aware of your thoughts, negative and positive. Consciously affirm the huge spectrum of variables available to you and carefully select your options. There are situations predestined that occur many times in our lives. But no matter how limiting they seem at that time, there is always a possible outcome that will be good for you in the long run.
The challenge is finding it. It is like a carefully designed puzzle.
Think of it this way; if everything were easy and obvious, your life would not be the romantic and gloriously exciting adventure that it is.
Finding the inner peace while experiencing life's ups and downs will help you magnify and awaken the power of your spirit.
Become aware of the endless possibilities and expand your horizons.

INNER CONVERSATION
"I am aware of the eternal indestructible power and timelessness of my spirit.
I will look deep into my soul and follow the guiding inner voice
towards a new adventure."

EXERCISE

Find a comfortable and quite place. Relax and breathe.

Visualize yourself looking at the night sky. The moon is shinning brightly, it I almost full. There are many stars that twinkle across the horizon. The beautiful patterns that they design are majestic and unreachable. Now concentrate on a particular star in the sky. Watch as it twinkles and seems to have a life of its own. It is part of the perfectly designed night sky's tapestry, yet beautiful in its own splendor. Suddenly the star glows stronger and brighter than the rest and seems to be getting nearer and nearer towards you. Within moments it is so close that you can see it's surface. It is a beautiful golden planet. An unseen force is pulling you towards the surface of this unknown world and you find yourself floating in the sky nearing this planet.

You landed. The planet's surface is covered with sparkling golden sand. Feel the sand in your palm and allow the little grains to gently slip thru your fingers. Take a walk. In the distance you see a golden pyramid. Within moments as quickly as you think it, you are in front of it. You notice a beautiful entrance. You enter the golden pyramid and find yourself in a large dimly lit room. In the center of the room is a lovely ornamented golden chair. Take a seat. Serene music is playing and otherworldly yet familiar aromas fill the air. You mind is still and relaxed by the environment and you notice your body entering a state of deep relaxation. Suddenly you hear your inner voice asking you about your biggest desire in life. Take a moment and think. The moment that the answer becomes clear to you, a large screen appears before your eyes and you see yourself in the precise situation that you wished for.

It is so real it feels as if you are there, breathing, touching and living it.

Any desire that you have and crosses your mind becomes your instant reality. You know now better than ever the power for realization of your soul's desire. You take a deep long breath and within an instant you find yourself back home on Earth. Your sacred golden planet, the pyramid and the hall of realization are always there for you to visit. In a moment's time you may return and practice the instant realization of your dreams. Just send out a thought vibration with a perfectly designed picture, feel it, taste it, smell it, touch it and know that endless possibilities are yours to have and to hold.

AFFIRMATION
**"My spirit knows no limitations and can overcome any obstacle.
Anything my soul desires and is in accordance with the divine plan
can instantly materialize and become my reality.
The power of my soul is the power divine."**

JOURNAL

In this chapter you will remind yourself of the endless possibilities that are available to you at all times.

Note what unfulfilled desires you carry in your heart.

Visualize fulfilling them and include them into this exercise.

Look outside of the world and rules you've created that limit you and prevent you from experiencing your dreams, and expand your confidence.

Repeat this exercise and note how it has affected realization of your dreams.

Be patient, clear and persistent.

PART FIVE

Prosperity of Your BODY

24. PRESERVE AND APPRECIATE

Your eating habits reflect your state of mind, body and spirit. Providing healthy nutrition is a key element in staying healthy, happy and productive.

Your nutrition affects your entire being and your health, energy level, capacity for concentration, reproduction and sleep to name a few.

When you are healthy, you are very wealthy. One can not buy health. It has been given to you and is there to take care of, appreciate, cherish and enjoy. Your body is like a fine tuned instrument, tremendously complex and designed to perfection. Your sensitivity to the energy around you influences, transforms and guides you. Awareness about your environment is essential when you want to preserve the healthy body that was given to you.

Have you ever paid attention to a flower and how sensitive it is to light, water nourishment and love? Any regular houseplant will respond to your vibration, attention and love towards it. When given proper care it will flourish and prosper. Every living creature longs for and needs love and nourishment.

How often do you take time to pay attention to your body and really appreciate all the special gifts it has to offer? Proper diet, exercise and rest are key elements that your body needs. Fresh, vibrant and healthy diet that includes plenty of organic vegetables, fruits and water will keep your body healthy, strong and free of toxicity. We all know to avoid sugar, gluten, junk & fast foods, overly acidic foods and keep to alkaline food diet.

Above all, within the healthy food parameters, awaken the inner awareness of what your body needs. As we are all different, some of us do not eat meat, while others do, it is important to pay some attention to your individual needs and create the prefect diet for yourself. Discover what healthy foods you like. If everyone in your family is a complete vegan, yet you have a craving for eggs, maybe you should give it a try and see how your body responds. Maybe it needs that particular nourishment. You can learn to respect someone else's desire to eat a steak, if that is what they need. If you crave a certain kind of food, do your best to provide your body with the healthiest option to satisfy your craving.

Do not let the environment or social eating distract you from what your body's favorite appetite is for. Late diners and stress eating are other factors that need to be addressed. If you must eat a late diner, make sure it is very light and follow with plenty of fresh water. Stress eating is a bigger challenge. The best option is to surround yourself with nothing but light and healthy foods, like fruits, nuts and vegetables, so that when you must have something to eat, it is at least healthy for you. If you can control what food you have in your home, then your healthy diet will be much easier to sustain. It is certainly healthier to eat an entire basket of grapes and apples than a bag of potato chips and cookies. No use attempting to keep a healthy diet, if the food you have at home is far from it. So the first step is, controlling your food purchasing habits. I am sure many of you are familiar with the food shopping experience when you are hungry. You want to buy everything in sight, healthy or not. Upon return, you realize that you don't need or want half of things your purchased. Use self control and discipline. Teach others in your household to respect your needs for healthy food. Be an example so that they too may follow your healthy habits.Make a list of healthy, vibrant food you should buy, before going to the store. That will help you focus and stay within those shopping parameters.

It is quite challenging these days in large supermarkets since all food that is far from healthy for you is packed in very attractive packaging. Often you never even see the actual food that you buy, but only the packaging. If you would see the food without the box, chances are you would never buy it at all.

So strive to buy the food you can actually see, and be aware that some foods - even healthy- may not agree with you.

It will help you make the first step towards a healthier eating style.

INNER CONVERSATION
"By taking care of my body lovingly and providing healthy and fresh nourishment I will consciously appreciate its amazing qualities and beauty."

EXERCISE
Find a calm and peaceful place to relax. Breathe long deep and slow.
Visualize a large orchard. There are beautiful trees everywhere. Most glorious fruits are basking in the sun. Choose a tree of your choice, anything you desire. This orchard grows every tree imaginable, from tropical fruits to apple, peach, orange and any kind of grapes you desire. There is a special area with nothing but berries. They are ripe and luscious ready the tasted by you.
Think which one appeals to your taste. Which fruit seems most beautiful and irresistible to you? Pick one from the vine or branch and taste it. Do not rush but enjoy every single moment of it. Notice the texture, taste, smell and energy each fruit has to offer. Become aware of the pure energy entering into your body.
Pure clean and healthy energy that Mother Earth has to offer.
Relax and thoroughly enjoy the experience.
Repeat the exercise by visualizing vegetables. Remember which vegetables you like the most. Make sure you get them next time you go shopping for food.
Repeat the same exercise that you visualized by slowly consuming and enjoying every bit of the real fruit once you have made your selection.

AFFIRMATION
**"I sense what nutrition my body needs and wants.
I am in tune and provide perfect nourishment
for a strong and healthy body."**

JOURNAL

Note your favorite foods and what you eat each day.
Honestly observe how much healthy nutrition you provide for your body.
How is your energy level, emotional state and overall confidence and satisfaction about your physical appearance?
If you could improve anything with your weight what would it be?
When do you have a tendency to eat and what is your eating schedule?
Make a list of healthy nutritious foods that you are missing in your every day diet.
Review your food supply and note how much of that healthy food you actually have and what is the rest of your food supply.
And lastly make a health food shopping list. Review your nutrition in a week's time and note the improvements and deep unhealthy eating habits that will take longer to brake. With patience and discipline create a new healthy diet regimen and note how that affects your mood, energy level and self-confidence.

25. EMPOWERING RELAXATION

Don't you admire those people who always seem calm, centered and relaxed, no matter what their circumstances?

What magic recipe do they follow, how do they do it, what is their secret?

Can you have some of it, can you learn it?

Yes, you can.

Pay attention to your daily activities, people and environments and how they affect you. If stress is in your veins the minute you enter your workplace, then preparing yourself ahead of time is required. If a certain person is the cause of your anxiety, be aware. And if it is an activity that surely brings unrest to your being, acknowledge it.

How do you prepare for these challenging situations?

By empowering your energy field before you become vulnerable and exposed to the energy draining situations or people.

Your power and your strength need to be at maximum capacity. Have you ever experienced a situation that was exhausting? Maybe someone or something has upset or frightened you? Suddenly you were disheveled, weak and tired. What was the main cause for your depleted state?

Very often you were simply lacking energy, and had no strength whatsoever to stand up for yourself and fight.

Proper rest is essential for your overall health and stamina.

There are times when we do not know what is coming our way and are not aware of stress or even possible dangers awaiting us. But by being rested as much as possible, you are not going to be easily overwhelmed.

Many of us may feel energized in the morning, but thru the course of the day, our energy seems to have vanished. The day is merely half gone and we are ready for a nap. How often do you feel a need to take a nap and yet you refuse to rest even for a few minutes? Your productivity will no doubt increase, if you take a break and truly rest for a short time instead of ignoring your body's humble request and function at barely half speed. When you recognize your state of much needed rest, you must create a time and space that you can recharge your body within moments. Herein lies the secret. Relaxation and rest are required. You do not need much time. As much as fifteen restful minutes will completely refresh and relax you. No need for a long sleep. Living in today's reality where time is a luxury, you can achieve a recharged and replenished state within a short time. The key is, knowing when to listen to your body. If your day seems to be going on forever and you don't have a singular possibility to relax until you return home, then take that much needed break immediately upon your arrival home. Afterwards, you will have energy to enjoy your evening and be productive if you choose so.

INNER CONVERSATION
"I want to feel rested and energized. My low energy level can be replenished quickly. I will learn how to listen to my body's needs for rest and relaxation."

EXERCISE
Find a calm and quiet place where you can lie down. Relax and let go completely of any wondering mind activity, instead, concentrate on your body.
Breathe in long, deep and slow and slowly exhale. Repeat a few times.
Now ask yourself:
"Do I need to rest right now? Would it feel wonderful to lie down for 10 minutes, close my eyes and completely let go of everything that is happening at this moment?"
Listen to your body's honest answer. If your inner voice is sending you a confirmation, immediately respect your body's request.
Before you let your mind take over why you should not or could not take a break, close your eyes and take a nap for at least ten minutes.
Afterwards notice how refreshed, energized and peaceful you have become within such a short time. The key element is to listen to your body and respect it's rightful demands and needs. If you tend to ignore your body's voice and requests for too long, a chronically depleted feeling and overall state will come over you and it will take you much longer to replenish and make up for all the lost rest.
If you worry you will sleep too long, set an alarm clock for ten to fifteen minutes. You will be refreshed and relaxed upon awakening.

AFFIRMATION
"My body needs a break to replenish every cell and feel rested and alive. I recognize, listen to, and take care of my body's needs for rest."

JOURNAL

Note your usual state of energy. Do you tend to be often tired, depleted and feel like you could sleep for days?

Note at what time during the day does this feeling come over you.

Does it have to do with a particular situation or a person that instantly exhausts you? Do you need a lot of coffee to be able to get yourself together in the morning and function at all?

What do you do when you feel tired?

Do you eat something sweet?

Do you ever listen to your body when it asks you to rest or do you wait till late at night before going to sleep?

Can you allow yourself to rest regularly if you need to?

After practicing this exercise, have you noticed you have more energy?

Did you continue to have a productive day or evening?

Did someone now or in the past accuse you of laziness if you took a nap?

Pay attention to all elements that influence your behavior and relationship with yourself.

26. INVIGORATING EXERCISE

Exercise is like required maintenance for your body. What is your individual preferred physical activity? Some of us need more vigorous workout and others prefer easy stretching and long walks. If you are the kind of a person who needs to be motivated for physical activity, you may join a local gym or yoga studio and create a regular daily routine. The environment and other people exercising will most likely help inspire you to participate. If it seems just impossible to get going, and working out seems like a gigantic struggle, create a habit where you reward yourself with a small treat for exercising. Of course that does not meant that you will be devouring a huge chunk of chocolate as soon as you are finished, but maybe give yourself the luxury of complete rest afterwards, a half an hour reading of your favorite magazine or book, relaxing in nature and just being still, without any pressure.

Or perhaps start writing a journal of self discovery. Each day after working out, write a few sentences and talk - write to yourself as your own best friend. Whatever is on your mind, your questions, worries, desires and feelings. Put them down on paper and take a look at them. Maybe they just need to be released and as soon as they are, they loose power and do not pre-occupy you any more. After physical exercise you will undoubtedly feel better, calmer and more focused therefore this is a great time for self reflection.

While you were exercising a certain part of your mind had to concentrate on your physical activity, so your mind got relieved from "thinking overload" for a bit. Now you can enjoy a peaceful but invigorating state of mind.

If you are uncomfortable with group classes and want to exercise at your own pace in the privacy of your home, you may acquire a video that you can follow along or a book that will guide you thru a workout segment. Yoga might be the answer if you want to concentrate into asanas- yoga positions and stretch at your own pace. Select an easy to follow style and take on more challenging positions as you go along. Do not set such high standards and be so demanding with your body that after one try, you will not only get sore muscles, but also become completely discouraged. Be gentle and patient with your body. It needs some time and practice to be supple as you desire. Keep in mind, that we are all different and the point of physical activity is not to compete how limber your spine is or how far you can run. Many yoga classes nowadays seem to have landed on a purely gymnastic level. It does not mean that you are enlightened, if you can stick your foot behind your neck. It merely means that you happen to be flexible in hips. When you practice any physical activity with relaxed and mindful concentration you will achieve a calm state of meditation. That combination will do wonders for your soul, body and mind. You will start enjoying the routine and will become a different person. It will be you and your running, swimming, yoga or gym workout. Whatever it is, when you find a sense of inner peace at the same time, you have succeeded.

Healthy and proper breathing must always be practiced when exercising. Concentrate on inhalation and find an even rhythm within the movement. Think logically. When stretching upward you are not going to be exhaling - but inhaling, and when bending forward you should not be inhaling - but exhaling. Become aware of you body and the comfort zone it needs. Be in synch with it and enjoy all that it is capable of. Keep in mind we are all different and have different qualities. Some of you can run forever, some can stretch with ease. No one is better; we are all different and unique. Be patient with your body, push it only as much as it will let you and reward it with attention and proper rest. In return, it will prosper and reward you with strength, flexibility and physical power that will magnify your self confidence, inner happiness and peace.

INNER CONVERSATION
"I am determined to find an exercise routine that suits and motivates me.
I have within me the perseverance to start, continue and learn how to
enjoy the great strength and power my body wants to experience."

EXERCISE
Visualize a beautiful green grass meadow. It is summer, the sun is shinning and there is no one else there but you. You are healthy, light and full of energy. Breathe in the fresh air and stretch your body. Inhale deeply and go for a run. Light as a feather, with tremendous ease you are running thru the meadow.
It feels wonderful and every cell of your body is alive. You are fast and can run tremendous distance without any effort. Concentrate on your calm breath.
You can run as far as your heart desires, and you never tire out. Run to the edge of the meadow and find yourself on a beautiful empty lake shore. Do you feel like going for a swim? Effortlessly jump into the water and swim out into the open. Breathe, and enjoy the lightness of your entire being. Every more is performed effortlessly and easily. You can swim as far as your heart desires and never feel tired. Your body is strong and in great shape. Now you return to the shore and sit down on the sand in a comfortable position. Close your eyes and enjoy the compete stillness and inner peace. Your body feels refreshed, rejuvenated and toned.
Repeat this visualization every day before exercising. It will remind you how wonderful you are going to feel afterwards and will help you avoid laziness and resistance to exercise. Remember, it is not work, it is fun, play and power for your body.

AFFIRMATION
**"I enjoy movement and amazing power my body generates when I exercise.
I am keeping the muscles supple and strengthening my structure.
I can feel my body gaining physical strength and power".**

JOURNAL

You know better than anybody when it's time for a tune up. Today is the prefect day to begin with your new routine. When you have decided what your physical activity is going to be, set your mind to it and do it. Note how you physically feel before embarking on this new program.

How is your energy level, appetite, frame of mind, self confidence, sexuality and love life? Do you feel attractive, healthy, full of energy, and positive?

Do you feel like it is too late and you will never again feel fit? After you have exercised answer the same questions. Keep a diary and follow up each time and observe how your physical activity affects your entire outlook on life.

Now you know the positive effect this new exercising habit has for you. It is never too late to change your disposition towards your physical self. Create a new you.

27. CREATING AN AGELESS BODY

Your aura is the delicate, invisible, and sensitive subtle energy field that surrounds and permeates your entire physical body. High stress levels deplete you and your energy field. When you don't regularly rejuvenate your body and it's essential energy elements, you are using-up your reserves. With proper rest, nourishment, exercise, healthy lifestyle and environment you can recharge and revitalize your body, keep the energy level high and reverse the aging process. They say time is not on your side when it comes to aging. That is only true, if you keep depleting your body, not recharging it properly and living off your reserve power. Stress, unhealthy habits and not enough activity are your primary enemies.

Time is your friend. With time you can transform your beauty and bring it into a new ageless dimension. When you are healthy and full of vibrant energy your age is at a standstill. With time, outer beauty reflects your inner beauty more than ever. Keeping pleasant and positive thoughts, a worry free mind, and an open heart will reflect on your face. Wisdom and experience will add a special all-knowing glow and sparkle to your eyes and the beauty within will truly take over.

Often we see a young person who is not taking care of themselves, they are exhausted, undernourished, have a few unhealthy habits and their energy level is low. They fell passive and unmotivated. They may be young by their year of birth, but physically and mentally they feel tired, old and depleted.

Your youthful state has a lot to do with how you take care of yourself and your outlook. Are you content with your life on all levels and in various different aspects? Feeling ageless doesn't require your preoccupation with a young appearance. Enjoy your maturity and wisdom and take care of your body. Treat yourself as lovingly with care as you would your favorite person in the world that you adore and want the best for. Lovingly practice this simple technique every day. It will rebuild your vitality and become your anti aging routine. Breathing is essential. Daily breathing exercises will provide oxygen to every cell of your body, rejuvenate you, bring a healthy fresh glow to your face and keep you vibrant and youthful in body and mind.

INNER CONVERSATION

"I celebrate each day of my life and love my growing, maturing and blossoming experience. I love myself and my physical body that takes me anywhere I desire.
I embrace my ageless spirit and promise to take care and
nurture my being the way I would someone dearest to my heart.
I am ageless and will remain eternally young in my body, heart, mind and soul."

EXERCISE

This exercise can be practiced anywhere, while lying down, sitting or standing. It requires a few minutes of your concentration and will bring numerous health benefits to your body, energize your entire being and keep you agelessly beautiful and vibrant.

Close your eyes. Concentrate on your breath.
Breathe deep and long thru your nose.
Listen to your breath and still your mind.
Inhale and exhale deeply 10 times.
Now inhale and hold the breath for a few moments. At the same time concentrate on your feet and tense and contract all the muscles in your feet.
Hold for 5 counts. Slowly release the muscle contraction and exhale deeply.
Repeat three times. Continue thru each body part. Start with your feet, proceed to your calves, thighs, buttocks, lower abdomen, stomach, chest, shoulders, your entire back area. Now proceed to your hands, lower arms, upper arms, neck and shoulder area and finally face and head. Take your time and really concentrate on isolating each muscle group mentioned and tense and contract it while you inhale. Repeat each section three times and feel your body recharging instantly. All your cells are awakening and working. They feel alive and vibrant.

In the beginning you might realize how disconnected you are from your body. The muscles don't seem to want to hear you or feel lazy. Be disciplined and continue with this simple yet powerful exercise. You will notice how in a few minutes your entire body will awaken, revitalize, recharge and feel energized. This is essential for your ageless state. In order to keep youthful you must reconnect with, feel, activate, and recharge all your muscles every day.

AFFIRMATION
**"I am charging my body with eternal source of life, youth and beauty.
My every cell drinks the awakened life power
and illuminates my entire being."**

JOURNAL

Note how old you are and how old you feel.

Do you feel young at heart or have you stopped in time in a particular time zone?

If you feel younger than your age says, pay attention at what age you remained in your mind.

Go back and note what was happening in your life when you were that age.

Were you in love? Enjoyed great success? On a fun journey? Maybe just had a child? Remember that happy time and keep it as your energy booster.

What is happening in your life now that could evoke similar feelings?

If you can not find it, create it. It is one of the things that make you feel young.

Fall in love again with your partner, remember what brought you together, or if you are single, enjoy your freedom and all the possibilities it presents. Take a course in foreign languages or dance if that was your happiest time. Find a new creative project that will remind you how to feel passionate, alive and young at heart.

If your happy time is now, and you are in synch with your age, cherish, appreciate and be aware of your great life.

Being able to recognize and truly enjoy the present "happy time" is important. Practice this exercise and each time note how you feel afterwards.

Use the affirmation and note your change in your disposition towards your age.

Note any new self discoveries and know that the more content and at ease you are with your age, the closer you are to feeling and becoming ageless.

28. CELEBRATE LIFE ...NOW

Life and everything in it, that is beautiful in so many different ways, is meant to be celebrated. Your body is a gift from the divine. You may use it to live out your dreams and desires, travel to marvelous places in this world, and connect with other living creatures. To learn and experience life. To love and celebrate.

When was the last time that you thought of your good fortune? The fortune of being here and experiencing this life. Your life is full of possibilities and opportunities. Simple joy of living is something we should remember more often. The joy of waking up, seeing the sky above you and the loving people in our life. The joy of nature, laughter and moments of bliss. The joy of inexplicable beauty of a flower or a butterfly. The perfect harmony in design on its wings.

Life is beautiful. Life must be celebrated.

You might be surrounded by a large family or be a loner with a few houseplants to keep you company, no matter what the circumstance, you can celebrate life. How?

Remind yourself to stop and smell the roses, notice every little aspect of good fortune that you are privileged to have, see and enjoy.

Do you take everything for granted?

All the beauty that you have in your life, do you ever really pay attention to it? The beauty of being alive, going for a walk, and having a safe place to lay your head at night.

Whether you are surrounded by material riches or posses the bare necessities you can enjoy the riches of being you. Your body is a luxury.

If you learn how to pamper yourself, you will enjoy life in the simplest of ways. Celebration does not necessarily mean a big party with balloons and lots of noise. A celebration of life can be an intimate, quiet evening by yourself enjoying a bubble bath. Whatever your choice of celebration, letting your body know that you care, appreciate and worship it. It will bring you great happiness, peace, love, contentment and will enrich and empower your spirit.

INNER CONVERSATION

"I will pay more attention to the one reliable person that awakens with me every morning...myself. I want to pamper myself lovingly and with care. By respecting and celebrating my body, I will attract loving and caring people into my life and remind others to be the same way towards themselves."

EXERCISE

Find a peaceful and quiet place and relax.

Center your mind and sit in stillness. Concentrate and ask yourself what would be a fun, enjoyable and pleasant thing for you to give yourself as a present.

Make it a routine to enjoy your time for personal celebration once a week.

Here are some ideas of how to pamper your body and mind:

Take a bubble bath.

Sing yourself a song.

Give yourself some flowers.

Read a book.

Cook yourself a nice healthy meal with different foods - experiment.

Take yourself to a library, museum, cinema, theater, or a sporting event.

Pay attention to what events are in your area, maybe an interesting speaker that you would enjoy meeting will appear.

Write yourself a thank you note.

Draw a picture, create a decoration, garden - be creative with your hands.

Reorganize your favorite corner in your home.

Create a meditation space.

Learn a new hobby that you have always wanted.

Get a massage or a beauty treatment.

Listen to music and daydream.

Take a nap and let go.

Look at the clouds.

Go to the park or nature and observe the trees, birds, breathe and just be.

Take a short day trip.

Pamper your body's senses and celebrate your beauty.

Play your favorite game.

Do absolutely nothing, and daydream about the future you desire to create.

AFFIRMATION
**"I celebrate my life, my health, my body, mind and spirit.
I am grateful for all the blessings in my life now and always."**

JOURNAL

Note your level of your self-confidence before beginning with this exercise.

Do you feel attractive, successful, desired, appreciated, happy and full of joy?

Do you feel loved, cared for and protected?

Do you look forward to the rest of your life and the unknown adventures that await you?

After choosing and completing one activity, answer the same questions.

Do you notice a difference?

How so?

It is important to realize that you can create a loving and joyful environment wherever you are and whomever you are with, but certainly you are fine even by yourself.

Enjoy your peace and smile.

PART SIX

Prosperity of Your MIND

29. CONCENTRATE AND ATTRACT

If you want to create a prosperous life, you must first develop a prosperous mindset. When you are clear about what you want to achieve and can concentrate on it, it will come your way.

The route may be a bit different, but the end result that you envisioned will manifest.

Concentration of your mind is one of those skills we can not do without.

The encouraging fact is that anyone can learn how to concentrate.

But it does take practice.

The easiest way for some people to strengthen the practice of concentration is thru physical exercise. A simple yoga asana- posture may prove to be challenging to do. You cannot balance on one leg and that's it. But you will be surprised how quickly that changes once you set your mind to it.

Concentrate, breathe, be still and hear in your mind: "I am standing balanced! " The command has been given and if you keep that thought unwavering in your mind, you will stand forever.

If a person has poor concentration and cannot focus, it basically means that they cannot hold their mind in stillness. And when you can not hold your mind, you certainly can not hold your body in stillness.

If you force the mind to concentrate and affirm your strong command, the body will obey. Be tough with it. If you don't run your mind, it will run you.

You will be its slave, completely dependent on it and yet permanently on hold.

" What will my mind do and where will it go? A thousand things are flying thru my mind..." those are the words of someone who can not control their mind.

Controlling your mind and knowing what you want to do with it is very powerful.

We have seen magicians that make things disappear miraculously and sportsmen that define gravity. Their concentration skill is perfected.

Focusing your mind onto a specific subject, visualizing an outcome, sending healing energy to a person, or telepathically communicating with a friend.

All those activities require deep concentration.

Many times we say: "I can't concentrate".

That may be true, but just by saying that, you have influenced and weakened your capacity for accomplishing what you desire.

The power of words is tremendous and you must be careful and aware of what words resonate in your energy field. Do not say things you do not mean.

With regular practice of concentration exercises you will see fast results and be amazed at the changes your life will take. Never underestimate the power of your mind and your own power. Be confident and know that you too can perfect your concentration and become the master of your mind.

INNER CONVERSATION
"I want to be able to control my mind and decide what I think. I will be patient and confident and will learn to empower myself with this concentration exercise."

EXERCISE
Find a quiet peaceful place and relax. Breathe long deep and slow.
With each breath you are relaxing deeper and deeper and feel your body becoming heavier and more relaxed.
With your eyes closed, gently lift up your gaze as if looking far into the distance, just above the horizon, towards your Third Eye area.
Breathe and visualize a night's sky.
If you see the stars, go from one to the other and observe their shining beauty.
If you see sky without a star in sight, concentrate on the deep and endless space. Listen to your breathing and enjoy this amazing journey.
Nothing else matters, no other noise or thought can penetrate your mind.
Only the sky and the stars. Enjoy the space inside your imagination and the limitless horizon. Here you can see anything, replay all the memory footage you desire and create new reality. But for now, enjoy only the peaceful night sky.
Suddenly you see a falling star across the sky with a bright flash.
Make a wish, one wish, quickly without too much analyzing.
Breathe and release it into the universe.
Relax, breathe and slowly come back.
Open your eyes and know that your wish will come thru.

AFFIRMATION
"I have within the power of my mind the capacity to concentrate and create a new reality for myself and my loved ones.
I am concentrating and holding my mind completely still on the desired object."

JOURNAL

Note your state of mind before you started this exercise.

Was your sky filled with stars and did you travel from one to the next?

Did you see just empty clear sky and experience the vastness of the universe?

What was your wish? Did you see it clearly?

If not, what was distracting you?

Create a clear picture in your mind of what you desire and practice visualizing it.

You should see everything to the tiniest detail.

Do not leave anything to chance.

Repeat this exercise in a few days and notice the difference.

Was your wish clearer? Did the same thoughts disturb your concentration?

Make note and observe how with time, you will learn to hold your mind still on a desired object or theme, and improve your overall concentration ability.

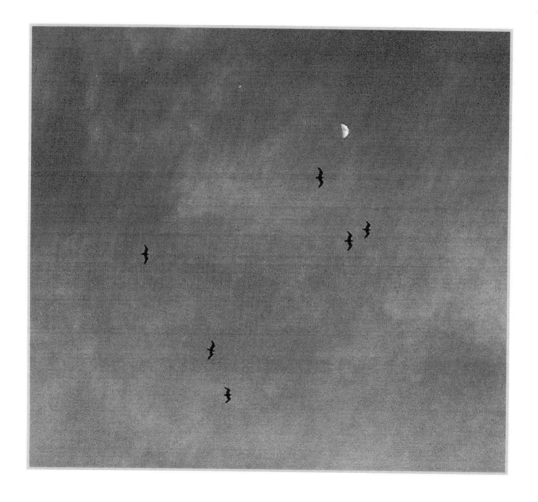

30. HEAR YOUR INNER GUIDE

Believe and you shall receive. Awaken and recognize your prosperity potential. Many factors need to be in place for successful and abundant prosperity.

Vision. Know clearly what you want or wish for.

Without a clear picture that you can visualize, you will not create a clear realty.

Belief and confidence. You must believe in yourself and your destined successful journey. If you are not confident and can not see yourself achieving a desired goal, you have not practiced prosperity in your mind.

Hard work ethics. Indeed, you can have brilliant ideas, but if you are not willing to lift a finger to bring them into realization someone else will beat you to it, by being faster and more disciplined. Finish your assigned work for each day.

Persistence. That means no matter how many times you fail, you do not get discouraged. Maybe you adjust and change your approach. Maybe you expand your horizon. Maybe you become open to what the universe has to offer. You wanted an apple, but the universe is offering you an orange. It is not exactly what you envisioned, but it s fruit and it tastes great. And as it turns out, you discover that you prefer oranges to apples.

Faith. This is a strong force that has gotten mankind thru many torturous and helpless moments. When it is a matter of life and death, faith and belief will keep you alive.

Positive mindset. When it takes over, do not underestimate the tremendous power of it. It will keep you going in the toughest of times and will keep you humble in the best of them.

Remember that everything in life can change quickly in less than a day. One call, one sentence, one second and your wildest dreams may come true. Believe. The self-confidence, faith and belief go hand in hand.

Are you weak or are you strong? Are you an optimist or a pessimist? Everyone is sort of a realist, because we all live in our own reality. Maybe you are convinced that you are a realist, when in fact your reality seems unreal to someone else. It works same the other way around. What is normal and real to me may seem impossible and unreal to you. One can never judge another, because you can not possibly know exactly how the other person feels, what they went thru to bring them here and what they feel, to behave as they do. Give some space to variables and know that to expand one's horizon is to expand your mind beyond the limitations of gravity, time and space.

Inner search occurs when someone or something changes our reality. Why, how, who, and what happened? Suddenly nothing makes logical sense and we embark on a deep search. If there are no obvious outside answers, we search inside ourselves. It is human nature to usually get to that point after a profound experience that awakens us. We realize that there is something inside us that knows all our deepest secrets, feelings and desires. That "something" or "someone" is the highest aspect of your soul. It is forever with you and it is sending you messages all day and night long. But do you listen? You could be listening a bit more.

You may get an answer any time.

When you find that inner voice, you will realize that anything is possible and everything is available to you.

What makes you different from anyone else who has unlimited abundance and prosperity in their life?

Your mindset and your circumstances my be different, but with a vision, faith, belief, hard work and persistence, you too can enjoy and create the limitless prosperity in all areas of your life.

INNER CONVERSATION

"I am aware of the abundance available to me. My higher power is always providing me with guidance and messages. I am going to tune in and listen."

EXERCISE

Find a peaceful place, make yourself comfortable and relax.

Breathe and relax deeper with each breath.

Calm your mind and hear only your breathing.

Visualize your desired prosperous outcome and situation. See yourself enjoying the fruits of your labor and successfully achieving your goal.

Now ask: "What is in my way? What is keeping me from succeeding?"

Be clear with your answer. Take your time. How can you eliminate this obstacle? Which way to go? What changes are needed? Who to contact or reach out to? How can you start? Sum up each challenge and package it into one clear question at a time. Concentrate on your most pressing question and visualize opening your mind like a powerful receiving antenna. It will catch any useful frequencies with the information you need and guide you into the right direction. It is very sensitive to signals that you will be receiving from now on.

Relax, breathe and remain internally alert.

Keep this feeling throughout the day as much as you can. Pay attention to every event in your day, all the people you meet and all the words you hear. Pay attention to the lyrics of a song that just came on the radio. Does it seem it was precisely meant for you to hear those words? Have you thought of a certain idea or desire and minutes later an opportunity came along?

All those seemingly meaningless messages or coincidences are meant for you to register and then use them sensibly. Hold the vision in your mind and let the universe guide you to the right situation and place in time so that you may continue on your predestined and desired path towards success.

AFFIRMATION

"I am listening to my inner voice and paying attention to all messages that I receive. It is clear to me how to connect all signals and find the right path to abundance and prosperity."

JOURNAL

Note how you feel about your state of abundance at this precise moment.
Ask yourself the questions in the exercise and note the answers.
Take your time and find honest answers.
Practice suggested visualizations and clarify and fine-tune your vision.
Note all possible interesting messages you observed throughout the day.
Does anything ignite a spark of an idea or solution in your mind?
Repeat the exercise in a week and note the changes and improvements.
Write down your inner conversation.
Develop a new habit of paying attention to and hearing your inner voice.

31. AWAKEN SELF-CONFIDENCE

The inner dialogue that you conduct in your mind has a great influence on every decision, action, feeling and outcome. Some of us have a tendency to listen to our minds, and some hear only the heart. Ideally one should balance these two strong voices and find the perfectly balanced answer and solution for every challenging situation.

What we allow ourselves to permeate the mind is of great importance.

Do you have a tendency to feel confident-thinking positive, encouraging words or do you feel weak and frightened in your mind?

Many of us who suffer from poor self-confidence have a tendency to blame someone else for it. Either it was someone in the far past, or a person that we have in our lives now, a situation or event, whom we believe robbed us of that inner confidence.

Your boss, your parent, partner, whoever it may be, they may play a role, but only as prominent as you allow. No one can take responsibility but you.

You can be aware of the influences, but do not let anyone else have control over how you feel about yourself and your personal power.

We do know that tremendous influences on our psyche happen in our childhood. So even if you find yourself at the present time in a difficult relationship where the partner is far from encouraging you, the source of the problem may be much older. Going into your past and discovering who, when and what exactly happened to you, might be difficult. Maybe you have simply erased the entire event and don't remember it.

But no matter what the past, a good time to address this issue is now.

If you can, talk to your parents, siblings or relatives and do some research. Casually inquire how supportive your parents were of your childhood dreams, ambitions and desires. The memories may return once you get some help.

Was anyone supportive of you? Did you ever get encouraged about your efforts and rewarded for your success? How abut your special talents? Everybody has a talent that they usually discover early on. Once you review your family set up, go back and remember your school teachers early on. Anyone special that understood you, recognized your gifts, and gave you an opportunity? Was there a difficult teacher who put you down and was unreasonably strict? All those tiny details matter and once you set your mind to it, you will remember. The details will come back to you like the pieces of a long lost but never forgotten puzzle. Discovering your past and what influenced your dispositions is most fascinating. Once you have unveiled a few mysteries and made sense of it all, you will experience a great release of old limitations. You will realize that all possibilities are yours and today is your first newly self-confident day.

Enjoy and remember, the sky is the limit.

INNER CONVERSATION
"I will re-set my memory and reawaken and empower the ability for self confidence that I have. I can decide for myself what I am capable off and will listen to my higher voice of knowledge for guidance."

EXERCISE
Find a calm and peaceful place where you can relax without any distractions. Breathe long, deep and slow. Concentrate on your breathing. With each breath you enter deeper and deeper into state of complete peace and calmness. Visualize a beautiful green meadow hiding deeply in a forest.
It is protected by large pine trees and completely secluded. Take a walk in the meadow and sense the grass under your bare feet. It feels comfortable and fresh. In the middle of the meadow stands a large flower with a huge flower bud. Come closer to the flower and notice the flower bud open up. Inside, sitting on the flower petals is a beautiful young child, sleeping. It wakes up and notices you. It is happy to see you. Lift the child off the bloom and take it for a walk. Ask the child its name, if it is happy, and how does it feel. Listen carefully to all the answers. Now ask the child what is its biggest wish. Take your time as the child thinks and gives you the answer. Does it think it is possible for their wish to come thru? If not why is it so?
Take the child back to the large bloom and place it back on gentle flower petals. Give it a big hug and tell it that anything is possible and it shall happen. Whatever you intuitively feel the child needs for self-confidence, say it from your heart. Promise that you will come back for a visit very soon again and will always come when you are called. The child will never be alone again. Now it looks content and happy. It closes its beautiful eyes and falls asleep. The flower petals protectively surround it and the flower bloom closes up.
You will visit this child again soon.

AFFIRMATION
"I am visiting my inner child to inquire how it feels, what it dreams of, and to help it develop the self-confidence that it has. This child is special, beautiful and has great powers. All its dreams will come thru."

JOURNAL

Note everything that the child told you. Remember every detail.

Repeat this exercise whenever you feel the desire to connect with your inner child. Note the different answers that you receive and how these realizations affect your everyday life.

The self-searching journey has many stages and this one is a very important link to your past. By returning to your inner child and encouraging it to be optimistic about the fulfillment of its dreams you are rebuilding a new habit into your sub-consciousness, so that you may develop stronger self-confidence.

Note the progress when you repeat the exercise in a few weeks.

Do not break this promise to the child. You must return any time it needs you, remaining reliable and dependable. Learn to hear that inner voice of your inner child and visit every time it calls on you.

32. MINDFUL PROSPERITY

What do you see in your mind when you think of a prosperous person?

Can you see yourself prosperous, abundant and successful?

Do you have a profession that brings you joy and fulfillment? Before you blindly chase a rainbow that you may not even like in the end, do some researching and inner searching. What do you consider a successful person?

Some of us usually have a role model or an idol. Maybe we found it during our teenage years and it has stayed in our minds as the untouchable, amazing person that we wish we could become or meet.

What is it that we like about that person? Do we know him or her personally and what do we know about their road to success? Do we know the price tag that came with that success? Are we familiar with only one part of their life, like for example career? And what happened in their personal life or do they have none? What happened once they achieved their goal? Did they share their success or get into usual self destructive habits?

Did they get involved with a charity, or did they forget all of their less successful friends and waste tremendous opportunity for helping others?

What choices would you have made where you in their shoes?

If you have dreamed of becoming a doctor and finding a cure for a disease, what would you do with that success and prosperity? Would you quit and feel satisfied and content or would you go on another long research journey and never take a break? Is it pure ambition that drives you, desire for material riches and fame, competitive spirit or the true joy of what you do and the wish to help others?

Whether it would mean making them laugh, teaching them, reading, or cheering them up with flower arrangements? Have you remembered to keep the joy and love for your calling or do you see only dollar signs?

Abundance of the spirit is the one to cherish most, and a truly abundant and prosperous person usually possesses the biggest riches in their enlightening ideas. Brainstorming with a friend who materializes their dreams into reality is always enlightening. People who have a giving nature will help us uplift and discover within ourselves same qualities.

Learning from a successful person can be interesting. We may also learn from their past mistakes and teach them something in return.

Who is successful at what you want to pursue?

How did they get there, what was their desire, circumstances and journey?

Become familiar with a person who has achieved what you strive for. Do some research and really get informed about the ups and downs of the profession. Keep in mind each one of us has an individual journey-you can not copy or recreate someone else's life. But you can learn from them.

Let's say you want to write a book. Have you ever written anything? Is there a purpose, a need for this book, a message, an entertaining story you want to share? Are you passionate about this project or is your motivation something else? Writing requires a lot of work and discipline and tremendous persistence-make sure you are up to the task. Maybe you want to have a restaurant. Have you ever researches how much time and effort this requires-every day and late into the night- all the time? Find out and get informed. Know what the life of a restaurant owner demands and what they have to sacrifice to keep everything going. Nothing happens overnight. Most often the ones who seem to enjoy overnight success have been at it for years, but no one else knew about them. What happened overnight was that others suddenly recognized what this person is about- but they may have been working at it for decades. Many girls dream of being a ballerina, yet do they possibly know of the sacrifice they would have to make to become one? The intense discipline, the long hours and years of training, physical pain and bloody blisters, competition, and short-lived joy of that profession? Suddenly you are not so excited about it anymore and the beautiful costumes and applause doesn't seem to outweigh the sacrifices.

Do some research and find out more detail about what is it that you want to do and the real future of it after achieving the your goal. Knowledge is power, so get informed and familiar with all the details of your life's calling. Follow your heart, and go in the direction that brings you joy and a sense of fulfillment. When your heart and passion is in your work, abundance and prosperity will follow.Research. Find out what is it that you would be willing to sacrifice, work at, and persevere to achieve abundance, prosperity and success in your life?

INNER CONVERSATION

"I know there is a special assignment that awaits me in my life. When I am on the right track I will experience inner joy, fulfillment and prosperous abundance."

EXERCISE

Find a calm and peaceful area. Breathe long deep and slow and completely relax. Visualize your role model standing in front of you. If you do not have a role model visualize a person who has achieved what you want to achieve. Commence a conversation with them:

Are you happy? Why did you choose this profession?

What is your life like? What were and are your sacrifices for this success?

What does it take to succeed in your profession? How long is the training and education? How many of prospective newcomers actually succeed?

Do you feel content or do you still want more? Do your old friends treat you differently now? When did you first know what you wanted?

Has anyone helped you or encouraged you? Do you have any regrets?

Continue asking your hero anything that comes to mind and listen to spontaneous intuitive answers that come your way.

Repeat the exercise in a few weeks after extensive research and continue mindfully but whole-heartedly on the road to choosing your path.

Set a realistic step-by-step plan for your journey towards achieving your desired success. Study all elements and situations required for success in that area.

AFFIRMATION

"I am discovering the details of my life's work and journey. This way I can make the correct choices for happiness, abundance and prosperity."

JOURNAL

Remember we are all unique beings and your road to success is special.

You cannot possibly plan and predict your individual journey, but you can prepare on many levels. Note the answers that you received from your imaginary role model. Write down your idea about success and what would bring your joy.

After research, return to your notes and compare. Is your motivation purely financial? Be honest and search for the perfect assignment that would make you happy, and has a great potential for your successful and prosperous future.

You will only enjoy destined success if the desire comes from your heart, and is never purely financially motivated. Then, your passion will be contagious.

33. YOUR DESTINED ASSIGNMENTS

Life happens while you're making other plans. Whenever I hear those wise words, they remind me of how easily you can "get lost" in your thinking. Your mind seems to have a certain plan. When things don't seem to go according to the plan, you panic and refuse to see the possibility that there may be another plan here, one that is actually much better than yours.

And what happens when the destiny forces you into a new direction, one you never dared to dream about? That is when life gets interesting and unique. You cannot possibly know all that is going to happen to you, all the opportunities that will be coming your way and all the people you will meet by "coincidence". You don't know your precisely destined path. Destiny has a lot of space and you are a very active participant in shaping it, weather you like it or not. You see, the fun part of life is, that you do not know everything about your future. That is one of those wonderful exciting things about being alive. Every day, your entire life can change. You may be one of those people who think:" Nothing exciting ever happens to me!"

Not true. There are many exciting possibilities waiting for you, especially designed for you. All you have to do is show up. When? At the perfect time.

So, do not get discouraged when you feel you showed up and nothing happened. It will. When you least expect it and when you've sort of given up. Maybe your faith is being tested. Maybe you need to be just a bit more ready. The possibilities are endless. But there it is, when you thought nothing exciting ever happens to you, you will get that marvelous surprise and your life will change in an instant. Sometimes these changes are difficult. In order to get you out of one seemingly comfortable situation, upheaval is necessary for your departure. Maybe your life has to get very uncomfortable in order for you to get the message, and turn in the right direction or open up, and embark on a new journey.

The possibilities are ever present and endless. It is very important to learn to live thru these changes with an open mind. A devastating occasion like loosing your secure job may be the best thing for you. A new opportunity may be waiting for you the next day. It is essential to keep your eyes, ears and especially your mind wide open. Hear, see and notice all the opportunities that come your way.

When you live in tune with your higher self, your life's journey becomes quite an entertaining and miraculous adventure.

Look for clues. You are supposed to learn certain things and everything is not going to be laid out on a silver platter for you. That would be very boring.

Pay attention to what happens when you have an idea or a question in your mind. If you are very clear about your inquiry, your answer will be almost instant. You might bump into the person that will provide the answer or lead you towards your next assignment. It may happen anywhere. Most life altering events and meetings occur at completely unexpected times and locations. It is very important that you are prepared for anything.

Let's say you have a dream profession you wish to pursue. And in this particular moment you seem very far away from fulfilling your dream. What would happen if today you meet the person that can lead you to that opportunity instantly? Would you know what to say, or do? Would you be able to realize that opportunity and have the self-confidence and the wisdom to take what comes your way?

Therein lies the secret to your success. Knowing yourself, what you want and being prepared for it. Not next week or next year, but today ......now.

Until you are ready, you cannot complain about it. And when you are ready, seize the opportunity and the world will become your oyster.

Be open and let yourself be surprised. That is one of the things that can and will make your life a very unique, exciting and a special, fortunate, fulfilling journey.

INNER CONVERSATION

"My life's journey is unlike any other. It offers many adventures and special gifts. I am open, prepared, and ready to fulfill my destined assignments and seize the opportunities that come my way. Anything is possible."

EXERCISE

Relax and breathe. Concentrate and listen to your breath.

With each exhalation feel your body relaxing deeper and deeper.

Listen to your breath and visualize standing on a beautiful beach filled with golden sand. The ocean is deep, turquoise blue, and powerful. Each time you exhale, a big wave rushes towards you. You feel calm and centered. Walk towards the ocean and let your toes touch the water. It refreshes you. Turn towards your right and go for a walk by the ocean side. After a while you come to a big door. Open the door and look inside. You see your entire life's past. See yourself from your childhood to today, all your hard work, sacrifices, accomplishments, good and bad experiences and the desires and wishes you nurtured and pursued. Look at all of it, take a deep long breath, exhale and close the door. There is a key in the door, lock it up and throw away the key far into the ocean.

Now turn towards your left and walk into the other direction by the ocean's side. After a while you come to another beautiful golden door. Open it and look inside. See yourself happy, healthy, smiling and doing what you desire and love most. Take your time and enjoy and absorb the feelings of complete fulfillment, abundance, contentment and soul satisfaction. Your dreams have come thru and you are gloriously happy. Keep that image in your memory bank. Now close the door, lock it and keep the golden key. It is yours now and always. Know in your mind and heart, that all your desires and dreams can be fulfilled. Trust in the divine plan and your perfectly designed life path. All is well; you are on your way. You may always return to your beach and look thru your door into the land of all dreams coming true. Know that is it forever there and within your reach. Practice this exercise when experiencing self-doubt, in transition, or when feeling uncertain about your future. See yourself clearly fulfilling your dreams in abundance.

AFFIRMATION
"I trust in the Universal power that guides me every day in every way towards realization of my dreams. I gratefully accept my life's assignments. My life is abundant and prosperous now and forever."

JOURNAL
Note the feelings you had about your past.
Any regrets and hopefully happy moments?
Note about what you saw in your future.
Were you clear and saw yourself happy, healthy and fulfilled?
Repeat the exercise in a few days and note the differences in your visualizations.
Has your vision of your future changed?
Be prepared for new opportunities and remember that timing is everything.
Notice the doors of opportunity that have recently opened in your life and observe your willingness to let go of the ones that keep being closed.

PART SEVEN

Prosperity of Your SOUL

34. YOUR SPIRITUAL WEALTH

We live in a material world. Visual distractions lead us to believe that what we can see and touch has value, for it symbolizes success and abundance.
But true wealth comes from within your spirit.
Peeking deep inside your soul and discovering your deepest treasures can be a life long journey.
There are many levels to your consciousness and many puzzles that are waiting to be resolved. Gradually and with time, we remember the knowledge, wisdom, and endless prosperity that is available to us.
Life seems like a long sleep where many dreams occur. You wake up and don't instantly know who and where you are. But slowly, lovingly and patiently the self-realization comes. Bit by bit and in sudden spurts, you have flashes of your spirit - self and the inner power. One day, you will inevitably experience the moment where all seems so very clear, easy to understand, and obvious.
But then you might doze off in ignorance again and forget that you are the child of the divine, always provided for and forever unconditionally loved.
You are never alone, but are connected to all living beings in spirit.
You complete the entire picture.
Whether you believe in reincarnation or not, your spirit is part of something ancient, immortal and indestructible.
Whatever your life's circumstances, the truth is that right now you know only this life- your life. You do not know how it is to be a person on the other side of the world, in a completely different setting than yours. But you are connected to them. If you were alone with such a person, and would spend some time with them, get to know them, become friends, you would feel protective, loyal and giving towards them. They would become a part of your life.
An interesting way to look at this is to expand your awareness and know that you are intricately connected to everybody, all us humans are connected, and we share this place and time.
You have something in common with each person alive today. We are here in this world together – now. The riches of this world were given to you to enjoy while you are here. But we must take care of them and think of people that are coming to live here after us…our children. The never ending circle of prosperity is available to everyone for we are all born equals. It is your birthright to be happy, healthy and prosperous. Take what is yours and erase the doubts that are prompted by your environment. Open your senses, awaken your intuitive spirit-power and let the forces of the universe guide you towards your deserved inheritance. True spiritual wealth is yours now and forever.

INNER CONVERSATION
"I will awaken the source of all prosperity that resides within my soul.
I carry an immense treasure of information, knowledge and infinite love
that can guide and help me every moment of my existence."

EXERCISE
Find a calm and peaceful place and relax. Breathe long, deep, and slow and feel yourself falling into a profound state of deep calmness.
Visualize yourself in an old castle. You are sitting on a beautiful golden throne in a large hall. There are people all around you. On your head is resting a jeweled crown and you are wearing a unique ornamented gown. Next to you is a tray with abundance of food and wine. You are the royalty in this court, you are well liked and your wish is their command. Today is a special occasion. You are deciding about the fate of a few people. The guards are bringing them towards you and explaining what wrongs they have done. You are sitting and listening.
Now they bring towards you a pauper dressed in rags.
His face is old and tired, and his body worn out from many years of starvation. The guard explains to you that this old man has been caught stealing.
You must decide upon the punishment.
But just moments before you do, your visualization journey ends.
Breathe and remain in a state of deep relaxation.
Now, visualize yourself in an old, small village. It is cold, rainy and dreary and you are dressed in torn rags. You have not eaten anything in days and are starving. Your feet are bare and in pain. You are walking past the small houses. The streets are deserted and you feel lonely, sad, and desperate. You take refuge at the front door of a house to escape from the wind and rain. Suddenly, you notice a basket by the door. It is full of food, but what catches your attention is a large piece of bread. You think for a moment then grab the bread and rush away. Just then a village guard comes your way, stops you and discovers the bread in your hands. You are accused without a chance to defend yourself and taken away by the guards. You are taken to an old caste. Your punishment will be decided by the king.
Just before you realize what's happened your visualization journey ends.
Relax, breathe and return back into the present time.

AFFIRMATION
"I am connected to all life and all human beings and send love, compassion, and non-judgment to all. This unconditional love is the greatest power and wealth I could ever need and desire."

JOURNAL

Note your feelings as the royalty.

Could you see how easily you could misuse the power that was given to you?

Would you truly understand the beggar's position?

Would you judge him harshly?

Would you believe that you are godlike?

Now note your feelings as the beggar.

Would you hate everyone wealthy?

Would you feel deserving of that piece of bread?

Would you feel that God has forsaken you?

Now distance yourself from both situations.

What have you learned about judgment, reality, belief and the power of circumstances influencing your choices and behavior?

Try to practice this exercise by placing yourself in other people's situation and honestly visualize your behavior in different circumstances.

Get to know who you really are and who you could become, if life would take you on a different journey.

Remember, true prosperity lies within the riches of your soul.

35. THE ORIGINAL PLAN

There is only one of you and no one else has an identical path in life. Your life's journey sometimes seems like a mystery. How would you feel if the truth was revealed to you? The possible truth is, that you chose this particular life to fulfill your desires, learn your life's lessons, overcome the weaknesses and realize your deepest dreams. Would all this make sense to you?

Would you blame yourself for poor choices, decisions or difficult circumstances? Life only hands you what you can handle. When you think you can not sustain any more of a challenging situation, you get a much-needed break. Have you learned anything? Probably yes. Are you later happy that you went thru that painful and difficult experience? Again, probably yes. For it has made you who you are, wiser and rich in experience.

Why not reflect upon your life like a perfectly planned puzzle? You have all the missing pieces and with time you will place them where they are meant to go. Every experience that happened to you has prepared you for the next step.

A learning curve, a growing lesson. You and your life.

When did this all start? As soon as you were born. If you have children in your life, you probably spend a lot of time with them, communicating with them and teaching them everything that you can. Do you pay attention to their individuality and the ancient wisdom that they seem to have brought with them?

Sometimes they will say such direct and meaningful things, that your heart will stand still. They will, without hesitation, pose you a question no grown up dares to ask, innocently look into your eyes and expect an answer.

A child knows a lot more that you think.

You were a child once and you knew more than you can imagine.

In a way you knew more than you know now. You knew somewhere deep in your soul what your journey will be. You knew what you wanted to do and you knew that it would happen. You never had any doubt.

Did you ever hear a child say:" I will be a fireman. Well, maybe. It probably won't happen..."

The answer is no. A child is absolutely sure that they will become a fireman.

Unless, of course, they have changed their mind about the choice.

But the choice of succeeding has never changed. To them it is absolutely logical.

Going back in time and revisiting your deep-set knowledge from your childhood can be a very healing and self-empowering experience. You too can go back and revisit that time where you were certain about your success. You were certain that whatever you choose, you would achieve, get and accomplish.

There were no doubts in your mind. Go back in time and find clues to help you see into your life's journey with the same certainty as you once had.

Remember and listen to your ever-present guiding inner voice.

INNER CONVERSATION
"I will go back in time and remember what my original and pure desire was when I was a child. I will find clues for my life's prosperous journey."

EXERCISE
Find a calm and peaceful place. Relax and breathe long, deep and slow.
With each inhalation you are becoming more relaxed.
Take yourself back to the time when you were nine years old.
Where do you live? See your room. Remember where everything is in your room.
Take a look at your books and table where you do your homework. Try to remember what is your absolute favorite food?
Can you remember a particular outfit that you adore?
Are you alone or do you have a sibling? Any house pets that live with you?
Favorite toy? See yourself playing. What is your favorite game? Do you have any friends to play with? Do you have a special area in the home or garden that you can play your favorite game? Are you happy? What is your biggest wish?
Do you like to read? Are you mischievous? Do you get into trouble?
What do you want to be when you grow up?
Remember everything you can, even if it seems silly and unimportant.
Were there other things you wanted to be before, or did you always dream of becoming this?
What is your biggest wish?
Does anyone pay attention to your wish?
Do they think it is interesting or do they disregard your voice?
Are your parents encouraging your dreams and desires?
What is your happiest time that you can remember?
What is the biggest punishment you received and what for?
Do you like to laugh or are you shy?
What makes you happy?
Keep that in mind and remember the experience that brought you much joy.
Relax and come back into the present time.

AFFIRMATION
"I can remember what my pure desire was when I was little.
It is a part of my life's mission to fulfill that old desire in part or in whole and enjoy the experience as I wished."

JOURNAL

Note the feelings you had as a child. Honestly answer all questions in the exercise. Think about your desires, wishes and dreams you had as a child.

Did any of them come thru?

What could you do now, to fulfill your old dreams?

Do you see a parallel or any similarity between you childhood dreams and your reality today?

Does everything seem impossible to you and why?

Take time for yourself and make an effort at least partially to experience your childhood dream.

Note how that makes you feel.

Be loving and patient with yourself.

Trust in the journey of your soul.

You can sense clearly in your heart where your happiness lies.

Promise yourself to follow this voice and always include it into decisions about your life.

36. A VISION REVEALED

By now you have experienced many visualization exercises.
Visualizing your future is like a practice for a desired outcome.
After you have mastered the art of visualization, you can graduate to the next level of awareness. Expanding your inner vision. One of the true riches of your soul is the ability to see far into the future, to sense and feel what is available to you. You might ask yourself, what is the difference between visualization and vision? Well, vision is your capacity to see the entire distant picture without guiding it. When you reach a high state of deep relaxation and high concentration, you enter a new field of extra sensory perception. Many interesting sensations can happen in this state and you can experience deep inner vision.

Have you ever suddenly had a vision of something you never really thought of? Yet suddenly for a matter of a few seconds you could see the entire picture. Having a vision can be a profoundly enlightening experience. It will take your breath away and you will never do it justice, when you try to explain and describe to others, what you saw.

A vision can be revealed to you at a most unexpected time, when you are relaxed and open to the divine messages of your soul. A great idea my come to you in form of a vision, or your own distant future will appear in your mind.

Deep inside your soul you will undoubtedly know, that this vision will happen and come to realization someday. It lies ahead in the future. It is destined to be so. We all wish we could have access to this special ability to receive visions. By practicing deep states of relaxation and meditation you will eventually get there. It is most important that you are patient, relaxed, have no expectations and remain aware.

When a vision is revealed to you, make notes, revisit the picture in your mind and try to unravel every detail that is stored in your memory bank.

It is like remembering a dream. If you play it back in your mind right away upon awakening, chances are you will remember a lot more than later in the day. No matter where you are and what you are doing, noting vision is very valuable. It may seem to you at the time that you will forever remember what you saw. But if you wait too long to take notes, the pictures will disappear into a foggy distance and you will miss the gift that was offered to you. It is as if the divine intelligence wanted you to get a glimpse into your possible future.

"You can go there, you can achieve this, and you must travel this road to complete your life's mission."

So you see, having a vision is seriously important when it comes to creating your prosperous future. Take note and work with the universe to experience, learn and achieve what you came into this world for.

INNER CONVERSATION
"I want to knock on the divine door and get a glimpse
of my prosperous future and my life's predestined journey."

EXERCISE
Find a calm and peaceful place and relax. Practice the deep, long and slow breathing and feel yourself sinking deeper and deeper into a state of complete relaxation.

Concentrate on your Third Eye and relax.

Ask yourself: what area of my life needs most help?

When you sense the answer, write it down and set on a journey of research.

From now on you are a detective.

You must find out everything there is to know about that particular topic.

If your answer was career, you will embark upon a journey of research regarding career. What careers are available to you? Explore every possible earning option in this area of interest. Go to the library, look online, inquire about a profession that interest you, and get as close as you can to the "suspect". "Suspect" being your career. When you come across anything that rings a bell or looks familiar or fascinating and interesting, slow down and research more.

Get as much information as possible and give your mind as many options to expand. Give yourself plenty of visual materials that will help you see clear pictures of what interests you in your mind.

If your are interested in receiving guidance ora vision regarding a desired relationship, become aware of your tendencies, dynamics, and consciously examine your expectations. Whatever the area that seems challenging to you, offer your soul as many reminders as possible to awaken the inner vision and trigger a self realization moment. Stimulate your imagination and widen the knowledge.

When you provide all that material and information to yourself, one day, when you least expect it, your vision will appear. The clues and reminders you found will activate the capacity for a true inner vision to occur.

AFFIRMATION
"I am expanding my awareness and am open to receiving a vision."

JOURNAL

Note every area that sounds interesting to you on your inner search.

Note all discoveries and observations you found.

Precisely analyze your case and pay attention to information, visuals or thoughts that persistently stay in your mind.

Note any ideas that come to mind, or memories that revisit you.

Be patient and disciplined in your research.

Return to this exercise in a while and observe the new developments.

What changes has the research triggered in your life?

Do you have a clearer understanding of your path?

Know that spiritual abundance is your birthright and when you are ready to receive your vision, it will appear. Perhaps it will be just a quick thought, idea, or visual picture-this is the first step. Next time, a clearer, longer, and stronger moment of vision will occur.

37. YOUR UNLIMITED SOURCE

Some of us live in constant fear of poverty. And some of us behave as if we have a never-ending supply of money and spend it beyond our resources. In either case, we have deep-seated issues about being, feeling and living prosperously. If you think about it, you don't really need much in order to survive. If you were stranded on an island, food and shelter for yourself and your family would be your main concern. The rest would seem unimportant and you would not have other, usual cares of this world. No credit card bills, big shopping centers and endless rent and mortgage payments.

Our world revolves around finances. How much money do you need, have and can afford to spend? How big of a home to have, what car to drive, that is the concern of a few. Then there is the other side of spectrum of large majority of population where sheer survival is an everyday concern. How to pay the rent, where is the next check coming from, how to keep going or afford a necessity like health insurance? And sadly, there are many homeless souls that suffer and walk the streets in hope of a generous hand. Many are enslaved with addictions and others are just utterly lost in this material world of ours.

One of the keys to a less stressful financial existence is simplicity. Simplify your life and do not overextend yourself when not necessary. Imagine you are someone else looking at yourself. Notice your reality with the eyes of a distant observer. Maybe your poverty mindset has kept you in a state that keeps your poor. Or your buying something you don't need is just a desperate effort to fill an emotional need. Many of us do not realize that individuals who seem very prosperous may have similar financial stress as others who seem to have nothing, just on an entirely different scale. The many material toys have a maintenance price of their own. Instead of coming up with a modest rent check every month, they need to come up with a crazy sky-high mortgage. The same headache, just different package. Of course they most likely do not have a problem with feeding a family. In either case, we cannot let the financial stress ruin our lives. Another interesting aspect is that when facing financial hardship, or a dry spell in your prosperity, only your true friends remain around.

Think about how you can simplify your life starting today. Often scaling down provides great relief and creates space for a new creative energy. All of us have access to the everlasting universal well of prosperity. You can drink from it any time and anywhere. Abundance in every aspect is at your fingertips. Your connection and attunement with your higher voice is essentially important for prosperity in your life. If you recognize that prosperity is really a giving energy current, your life will change instantly. When you are desperately holding onto something and are very attached to it, chances are you will have to loose it in order to learn a valuable lesson. When you learn to give from the heart, you shall receive from the heart as well. Your incoming energy current opens only when you activate the outgoing current. The current must flow in both directions. The energy of abundance and prosperity is connected to activity and motion. You give your energy and you receive energy in return. Weather that is a financial gain, a gift, a caring word or loving helpful gesture, the giving energy current is flowing towards you when you open and activate it. Release the fear, open up and give loving energy. It will return your way, magnified and manifested in the best way to help you prosper. There are no limits to the energy source; like there is no end to the power of the Sun. Above the clouds of doubt, it shines every day.

INNER CONVERSATION

"I am aware of the universal well of prosperity and abundance.
It belongs to every one of us.
The well provides for every soul and the access to it is always open.
I am ready to reconnect with the unlimited source of abundance and prosperity."

EXERCISE

Relax and breathe. Bring your mind to a standstill and listen to your breath. Visualize a beautiful garden. See yourself in this garden. You are surrounded with glorious flowers of all kinds. The colors are mesmerizing and there is life everywhere. Blooms of impeccable perfection are swaying in a light breeze and you are enjoying a sight of pure beauty. This is your garden. Take a walk. Observe the flowers and butterflies flying and drinking from various blooms. Smell the unique scent in the air. This indescribable beauty all around you is lush in freshness. There is abundance of beauty and life. In the center of this garden is an ancient well. Come closer and take a look inside. There is a lovely golden bucket close to the bottom of the well. It is waiting to be filled up. Lower it a bit so you catch some water into it. Now very carefully pull the golden rope that holds it and bring it up towards you. Now it is in your hands. The water from the well is pristine clear. There is a golden cup attached to the bucked especially for you. Take a sip of the water and quench your thirst. It tastes more delicious than anything you've ever tasted. Now you know that you will never be thirsty again.This is your well of prosperity in the garden of your soul.
It is a divine well that never dries out. The water supply is always plentiful.
All you have to do is find it, fill it up, bring it to your lips and drink.This exercise will help you connect with the consciousness of prosperity. When you feel a lack, know that it is only in your mind. Pay attention, be still, and you will always find your well of infinite prosperity inside your soul. The solution will be revealed.

AFFIRMATION
"I have access to limitless prosperity. I honor my soul's voice that leads me toward immeasurable abundance on all realms."

JOURNAL
Note how you feel about the state of prosperity in your life.
What does it mean to you and what comes to mind when you hear this word?
Do you consider yourself spiritually abundant?
Would you like to improve your state of prosperity?
If so, write a prosperity wish list. What changes would a fulfilled wish bring into your life? What can you do to make the first step towards improving your abundance and prosperity? Practice the exercise and note how spiritually empowered you feel when you consciously connect to that universal power of abundance. Repeat after a week and note all changes that have occurred in your life as a result in your state of consciousness.

38. THE POWER OF YOUR CHOICE

What is the dream and desire for your future?

If someone asked you who is responsible for your past decisions, would you admit to being the one? Would you take responsibility for all your choices? What about the present time? Isn't it your choice to be where you are, with whomever you are, and do what you are doing right now?

Yes it is. You are not just a helpless bystander watching your life go by.

And what do you think will happen in the future?

It will be again you, who makes choices, decision and co-creates the scenario. No matter how hard you try to escape and blame it on the set of circumstances, you must take some credit and also responsibility for it. Some have a tendency to take credit only for the good, courageous and successful actions and events of our life. And yet others seem to constantly blame themselves for everything that went wrong.

Do you think you are objective in giving yourself the credit for the good and taking responsibilities for less positive decisions?

No doubt, the circumstances play a large role, the co-players that you have in your life affect you, but the final choice is yours. No matter how limited the options, there will always be a few choices there. These choices are incredibly important. They make you who you are. They determine your future. They have consequences. The are registered in your soul's history.

Make the best choice that you can at any given time and watch your life unfold. Do the best you can one step at a time. Don't procrastinate and hide. Jump! But remember, that you can make your dreams a reality only if and when you discover how to overcome the limitations you have set in your mind.

Who makes the decisions? Do you know what you want? What is holding you back? Your own intuitive voice or someone else's controlling presence? Spend time with yourself and give yourself a chance to be heard. All you dreams and desires, what are they? Say them out loud, write them on a page and visualize them becoming a reality. Now you are ready to take charge and be the co-creator of your life and your future.

INNER CONVERSATION
"I will consciously make positive, harmonious, and healthy choices
for my abundant and prosperous future."

EXERCISE

Find a peaceful and quiet area. Relax, breathe long deep and slow.

With each breath you are becoming more and more relaxed.

Visualize yourself sitting on a chair in an empty room.

In front of you are three mirrors. You can see yourself in each one of them.

Look into the first mirror.

This mirror shows you the life you are leading now.

Your job, your family life, your love, your health, your finances, and your every day experience. See yourself in the morning. Review your entire day.

Do you have any joy in your life? Are you happy? Do you take care of your health? Do you have any peaceful time for yourself?

And ask yourself what will be different tomorrow?

Where do you think you will end up if you continue on this road?

See the picture and close your eyes.

Now look at the second mirror.

This mirror will show you the life you will have if you play it safe and please others. What does everybody want and expect of you? How many obligations do you have? See yourself giving the control over your life to others. How do you feel? Are you resentful and disappointed in your own weakness?

How is your health? Do you ever smile? Are you happy?

Where do you see yourself if you continue in this road?

See the picture and close your eyes.

Now look at the third mirror.

This mirror will show you how your life will be if you follow your deepest dreams and desires.

What are you doing? Who is in your life? Where are you?

What is your day like?

Are you happy and if so, what makes you happy?

How is your health?

Do you share your happiness?

Do you help others?

Where do you see yourself in the far future if you continue on this road?

See the picture in your mind.

Close your eyes and relax.

AFFIRMATION

"I am aware of the power of my choices and make them from my heart, with my mind, while I listening to the voice of my soul."

JOURNAL

Note the experience with the three mirrors. Answer the questions about the three mirror parallel life choices and observe the difference.

Now on a new page create a perfect mixture of incorporating necessary elements of all three imaginary lives. Create a version where you follow your heart and your dreams, are able to fulfill any responsibilities you may have to others, and incorporate the reality of your present life situation and circumstances.

Create a compromise where everything can be harmonized and prosperous.

This is the model for your new way of life.

Make small changes and incorporate these ideas into your everyday.

After a few weeks note the difference in your enthusiasm and feeling of consciously participating in your life's journey. Now, you are an active participant.

PART EIGHT

Protection of Your BODY

39. ACTIVATE YOUR PROTECTION FIELD

You have no doubt experienced a time when you were in grave physical danger. Maybe while driving in your car, walking on your own in a dangerous area or living thru a natural disaster.

There are circumstances in your life where it seems that danger is unavoidable. Instead of giving into fear and feelings of helplessness, you can improve your situation with a simple yet powerful technique.

The electromagnetic auric field that surrounds your body is your energy shield. It absorbs vibrations that surround you and reacts accordingly. If you get frightened, your third chakra center connected with those feelings will react and close up. If you're in love it is most likely that your fourth-heart chakra will expand and connect with the etheric energy of your lover. If you are speaking in public, your fifth chakra will become more powerful-the center of your communication. When your mind is alert, your body's energy can be redirected and guided. Consciously connecting with your energy centers is the key to activating and magnifying the energy protection shield – your aura.

For example: you are about to embark on a journey. Traveling can be anxiety ridden. The crowd you encounter at the airport or train station can be overwhelming. It takes a certain frame of mind to get ready to face that kind of environment. Living and working in a big city carries its own disadvantages. Bumping into people on the street and in the subway disturbs your body's energy balance. Driving to work on a crowded highway has another aspect of energy tension. A noisy and crowded shopping center can energetically drain you. When you consciously prepare for it, your body's energy field can easier withstand an unharmonious situation.

An important fact not to be missed is, that when you take a shower, you cleanse your energy field. Your aura is more sensitive, receptive, and vulnerable to outer energies for about an hour afterwards. It is best not to immediately rush into a draining or unbalanced environment. Make a habit of giving yourself some time in peace when preparing for your day. You will notice that everything will be much less stressful and you will experience a higher energy level and productivity. Take a few minutes for this exercise before rushing out the door in the morning and create a powerful energy field around your body.

You can practice this exercise first thing in the morning or any time during the day when you feel your energy field weakened.

You will create a strong protection energy field around your entire body that will help you sustain and preserve energy.

INNER CONVERSATION
"I am taking this time to revitalize my auric field.
I am opening and activating my energy centers
and magnifying my natural protective power."

EXERCISE
Relax, be still and concentrate on your breath.
Still your mind, listen to your slow, deep and calm breathing.
See your body in your mind.
Visualize the first chakra and its color red. Inhale and see the chakra expand and vibrate with red color. Exhale and relax. Repeat three times. Move onto the second chakra and visualize it expanding with the color orange. Inhale and expand the color in that area and exhale. Exhale and relax. Repeat three times. Next is your third chakra in the solar plexus area and the color yellow. Inhale deeply and expand the area vibrating in beautiful yellow color. Exhale and relax. Repeat three times. Now move into the heart center - the fourth chakra and its color green. Again inhale and visualize expanding the heart area vibrating with color green. Exhale and relax. Repeat three times. Move into the area of fifth chakra – your throat. Inhale and expand the area while visualizing color blue, vibrating and energizing your throat. Exhale and relax. Repeat three times. Now center your concentration in the area of your Third Eye. Inhale and expand the area in the vibration of color purple. Exhale and relax. Repeat three times. Now you've arrived to the area of your crown center - the seventh chakra. Here lies your connection to the Universal power. Inhale and expand that area while visualizing clear and protective white color. Exhale and relax. Repeat three times. Now expand the white color all around your body. Inhale deeply and expand the brilliant, glowing, white shield of protection. Exhale and relax. Repeat ten times. Each time expand and vibrate your white energy protection shield.
An invisible shield of protective energy current now surrounds your entire being.

AFFIRMATION
"I am protecting my body with the energy that is connected to the
universal power. I am protected and safe."

JOURNAL

When you find yourself weakened at any time during the day, repeat the entire exercise or only the last part of visualizing the white light only and recharge your etheric protection field.

Note how that affects your overall feeling.

Repeat the exercise whenever you need and note how helpful this technique is for you.

Make it a daily habit that helps activate and magnify your energy protection field. You can use this exercise first thing in the morning, or each time after shower or bath.

For better, soothing, rejuvenating and relaxed sleep, practice right before bedtime.

40. SENSING ENERGY

We have all had experiences where without an apparent reason we felt a strong desire to leave the place, room or area where we are.

Did something happen?

No, nothing happened and nobody insulted us. Yet, we had to go.

Why? Something felt very uncomfortable and uneasy.

Often we hear stories of survivors, how moments before a dangerous accident for no apparent reason they felt an overpowering urge to leave or change their plans. It was as if an inner voice told them to get away, as soon as possible. They may have been the last person to leave that place alive.

How would you explain that? Coincidence? Chance?

None of the above. Many factors are at stake when our life is spared and saved, or miraculously protected from something dangerous or negative. Being in tune with our energy body is one of them. Listening to feelings of unease and physical discomfort connected to a location are warning signs.

It is wise to listen and even wiser to perfect that special gift that we all have. Being aware, alert, in tune and attentive will help you achieve that state of high attunement with your body that will always guard you, and drive you out of the danger zone in time.

When you learn to listen to your body's warnings of discomfort you are elevating your awareness to a different frequency level. Vibrations and unlimited frequencies surround us at all times. Just think of a radio signal. With a turn of the button you suddenly catch music frequency from thousands of miles away. Each day of our lives are increasingly more affected by signals. Fine tuning your personal receiver is a necessary ability you need for maximum protection of your body.

INNER CONVERSATION
"I want to understand the sensitive signals and messages that my body can send. I will awaken and elevate my awareness and increase my safety."

EXERCISE

Find a peaceful and quiet place and completely relax. Breathe long, deep and slow and concentrate only on the sound of your breath.

Visualize yourself sitting in a most comfortable chair.

You are warm, cozy and content.

Everything is perfect, you are worry free, happy and your heart is light.

Now you will communicate with your body about specific locations that you find yourself in at various times during the day. Your body will let you know how they affect you.

Let's begin: Think of your bedroom.

Visualize yourself there, concentrate and sharpen your awareness.

How does your body feel? Does it feel relaxed and comfortable? Do you feel anxious? Why? Does it have to do with your sleep mate? Maybe there are some old things in the bedroom that bother you? It is possible that the room does not feel harmonious and peaceful which is essential for a good night sleep.

Be still, concentrate and try to feel the source of uncomfortable sensation.

Remember the thought messages you receive, and now in your mind leave the bedroom, breathe and relax.

Now visualize yourself at your place of work.

See the environment, various objects and people that surround you.

How do you feel? Pay attention to where in your body you feel uncomfortable and what is the source of your tension?

Is there a person that negatively affects your energy state?

Is there an object that particularly bothers you?

Remember any messages, with now in your mind leave the place of work, breathe and relax.

You can repeat this exercise for any particular and also less familiar location.

Always be aware of your innermost delicate energy sensation and the source of any discomfort or the opposite; a sense of security, peace and tranquility.

Your body will energetically respond to your visualization.

AFFIRMATION
**"My body is a ultra sensitive device that informs me
of healthy and unhealthy locations.
It communicates with me instantaneously, warns me, and protects me."**

JOURNAL

Note how each selected location affects your energy body.

What makes you feel comfortable or uneasy?

Where in your body do you sense a reaction?

Compare this with the location of chakras and the emotions they correspond to. For example: an uneasy feeling in the solar plexus region is connected to feelings of fear and anger.

This will be very useful in your discovery of what and how certain places affect you. When you master the art of "energy warnings", you will be able to do this much quicker. For example; if you find yourself in a completely new location and want to know its effects on you, you will instantly bring your inner awareness into your body and sense how that specific vibration of that particular location affects you.

This will help protect you and avoid any negative environments you may encounter. Note your overall attunement with locations after you have practiced this exercise for a while.

41. CLEANSE YOUR ENERGY BODY

Negative emotions affect our health. They create an excess of energy that we keep within our energy body. That excess energy creates unease, the basis for dis-ease. Our "emotional baggage" is an unhealthy and energy blocking state. Some of us have a big amount of that baggage and we seem to be collecting more as we go along.

Have you ever traveled light? What joy! Your outlook on the entire journey is different. Nothing to worry about getting lost, no extra weight to pay for, and no sore bad back.

Many of us have difficult or challenging experiences that we can't seem to let go off. However, if we truly reassess and ask ourselves what is the benefit of holding on to the past, we can realize the answer is simple. There are absolutely no benefits! Keeping old and negative experiences in our consciousnesses only gives them more power and prevents new positive events from occurring, inspiring and uplifting our spirits.

When we release emotional baggage, we make space for new energy, people, and opportunities to enter our lives.

Often we may be holding onto old emotions we are not ever really aware of. We might feel uneasy, fearful or angry about a certain aspect of our life, but are not quite sure what is the source of it. If you suffered from a difficult and unhappy relationship experience, and are still holding on to that emotional state, you are preventing new people and relationships from entering your life.

How many times have you had the experience when you meet someone and they rehash the unhappy past with you until you become discouraged and overwhelmed with their baggage?

They kept the past negative energy disturbing the possibility of a new happy experience and prevented it from entering their life. There is no space for both. Live and let go.

Revisiting your past may be a good idea before this exercise.

It is not productive to simply ignore unresolved and unhappy emotions.

By addressing them and understanding their effect on your life, you can help eliminate and resolve them. Knowledge is power and knowing yourself will empower you. Develop a habit of releasing any negativity and maintaining peace and inner happiness. That is great protection for your physical health and emotional well being.

INNER CONVERSATION
"I am ready to cleanse my body of all negative thought patterns
and protect my positive energy field."

EXERCISE

Find a calm and peaceful place.

Breathe long, deep, and slow and completely relax.

Visualize yourself walking on a path, in the far depths of a beautiful rainforest. Lush, vibrantly green tropical trees and plants surround you. The narrow path is covered with small branches and leaves. The air smells fresh and moist. You hear a sound of running water in the far distance. It is mesmerizing. You sense it is calling you. You must find it. As you keep walking on the path the sound becomes stronger and soon you feel a refreshing fine mist in the air. You are coming closer and closer to the source of this immense sound and energy.

And finally there it is. You are standing in front of a beautiful, powerful waterfall. The sight is absolutely stunning. Without any hesitation you find an area where you can come right next to it and stand underneath a gentle stream of water. The water soothingly massages your body and cleanses your energy field.

Now think of any negative or upsetting emotion that you may be carrying with you. Visualize it as a small ball in your hands as you hold them under the waterfall. Sense them being cleansed, washed away with fresh water. The ball of negative energy is dissolved, vanishing. Repeat until you have cleansed off any excess toxic emotions that you carry with you.

This is your healing cleansing waterfall.

It can replenish you with vital energy and keep you ever charged with unlimited power.

After you have enjoyed your cleansing experience, you return back into the forest, rested and refreshed. You find a very comfortable area covered with tropical flowers. You lay down, completely relax, let go and take a rejuvenating short nap. Upon awakening you feel energized and happy.

You may visit this waterfall and enjoy its cleansing powers whenever you wish.

AFFIRMATION
**"I release all toxic emotions and let them be washed away
with the power of a waterfall.
I rest in the flower petals and awaken vibrant with a light heart."**

JOURNAL

Note any negative feelings and emotions that you carry with you. Make a conscious decision that you are ready to let them go.

Describe how you feel after this exercise. Has your overall state improved?

Do you feel cleansed of negativity?

Practice this exercise regularly and follow up with notating the results.

If you wish, repeat this exercise while in the shower.

Always review how you are feeling and continue to guard, cleanse, and protect your energy field.

42. RECOGNIZE THE ENERGY DRAIN

Our friends, coworkers, family members and loved ones affect our emotional state. When someone near you is depressed, chances are some of it will rub of on you. If you manage to cheer them up, you will most likely feel a bit depleted afterward.

We are all familiar with friends that call us whenever they seem to have a tremendous drama or lots of problems in their lives. After a long conversation, they seem to miraculously recover, and you feel exhausted.

Then there is the case of someone wanting to provoke an argument with you. They are moody and difficult, impossible to please or have harmony with.

After they successfully get you to react and engage in a confrontation, they suddenly lighten up and feel better, while they have spoiled your entire day.

Why do we allow others to affect us in such a way and drain us of vital energy?

Why do these people feel the need to release their negative emotions onto you and drink your life force? Obviously they do not have a self empowering capacity. Maybe they grew up in a family where the dynamic was similar.

Someone else drank their energy and they are now in return doing the same.

You can best help such a person, if you remove your supply of energy to them.

By forcing them to be self reliable, they will slowly recognize their weak state. Often sheer awareness of the habit will improve their behavior and make them face themselves and their fears.

There is the other side of equation as well. Some people light up the room when they enter, inspire us with a smile, a look, and a word, and positively affect our life in short amount of time.

Interaction with friends should be equal, you need to be heard and also offer a compassionate ear. Do not allow someone to continuously drain you while they lament only about their problems, never even inquiring about how you are.

Likewise, do not burden your friends using them to unload your grievances and ignoring their needs. Be aware of these dynamics and navigate them into a healthy dynamic and direction.

Certainly we should strive to surround ourselves with positive, giving and loving people who make us feel good about ourselves, and whom we can trust.

INNER CONVERSATION
"I am ready to eliminate draining people from my life.
I will be selective about the company I keep, and the energy I give."

EXERCISE

Find a comfortable and quiet place. Breathe long, deep and slow and relax your entire body. With each breath you are relaxing deeper and deeper into a state of complete peace.

Visualize yourself at the beach. It is a beautiful summer day and the sun is warm. You are going for a swim. You jump in the water and swim against the waves. The ocean is pretty wild, but you are an excellent swimmer and have absolutely no fear.

You are swimming far away from the beach and the water feels wonderful. Suddenly you hear a voice calling for help. Someone behind you is having trouble staying above water. Without a thought of hesitation you come to their rescue. They are not easy to save as they refuse to listen to you, are panic-stricken and hang themselves around your neck. With much difficulty and effort you get them to the shore. Finally you see their face. You know this person. It is someone you know very well, who always drains your energy.

And here again - they almost drowned you with their panic.

Remember who the person in the water was.

With the help of this exercise you can recognize who the people that drain your energy are.

You might be surprised for often someone who you hold dear and near also drains the life out of you. When we are too close to the situation, we loose track of the different dynamics. By being convinced that a friend seems to have constantly bad luck, we do not notice that the friend thrives on bad luck, and uses it as something to always gain your sympathy or attention with. Or they complain about their misfortune when in reality, they are much luckier than you. You could put a person like that in a room full of happy people and they would manage to gather a few victims around to get their attention and energy. How? By telling them their miserable story. Being aware of their habit, you can change it by simply making yourself unavailable, and limiting your time of contact with them. You will not give them the opportunity to drain you.

They will have to find someone else or face their bad habit.

Protect yourself by visualizing a bright white high wall of energy that protects you from the energy draining dynamic. Surround others with love and send them light. You will be surprised how quickly the situation will improve.

AFFIRMATION
**"I am aware and protected from difficult, energy hungry people.
By not responding to their need, I will help them
on their way to self empowerment and inner strength."**

JOURNAL

Note who the person is that first came to mind in the exercise. If it doesn't seem to make sense at first, maybe it is your best friend. Do not disregard them, but pay attention and make an effort to realistically look at your friendship. Are you the one always saving them, helping them and rescuing them from some saga? Are they around just when they need you, would they offer you as much support as you have given them, or are they taking advantage of you.

Honestly answer these questions and do not ignore the inner voice of truth that may be whispering something you do not want to hear.

Sometimes is it better to find out who is your true friend earlier than later.

Make a note who drains your energy in your life and who is an equally giving friend. You can correct the dysfunctional dynamics by gently removing yourself as their source of energy. If you do not enable them in their dysfunction you are helping them and re-establishing a healthy pattern.

43. HEALING AND REGAINING POWER

Our bodies have a tremendous capacity for self-healing.
We take that for granted and forget it.
Have you ever paid attention to a simple cut on your finger?
Most likely it healed itself within a few days.
Did it take any special effort or energy for you to do that? No, your body simply took care of it alone. Similar events are taking place daily within your body, yet you are unaware of it. When you feel discomfort or pain, your body is attempting to send you a signal that it has a difficulty with self healing in that region.
Therefore it is always meaningful to listen to your body's messages.
Our physical ailments tend to materialize in the energy field first. If we learn to keep a healthy and clean energy body, we increase our chances of staying healthy.
Emotional tension and stress affect your body's overall health. Regular and proper rest, a healthy diet, and regular exercise are the fundamental pillars of your health.
When you feel your body is depleted and is battling a possible ailment, you can use the power of mindful self-healing technique for speed-up recovery.
Pay attention to your body' signals and requests for help.
Give it whatever it needs, for it will guide you in ways so you can help it better.
When you'll do things right, you will feel well and when not - you will often experience immediate repercussions.
Maybe it is as simple as proper rest, or perhaps a change in the diet.
The biggest enemy of health is stress. If you've depleted your body's vibrant energy by exposing it to years of deeply stressful situations, a change in lifestyle may be necessary. Do not wait for a convenient opportunity, act now.
Assist your amazing body when it needs you, and appreciate your body's self-healing mastery.
Respect your body and remember to lovingly care for it, so it may help you travel the world and experience new adventures, happiness and joy, and help others lead a better life.

INNER CONVERSATION
"I will listen to my body's request for help and mindfully assist it to self-heal.
I want to feel healthy, strong and full of power."

EXERCISE

Find a calm and peaceful place. Breathe long, deep and slow and completely relax. With each breath you are becoming more relaxed and soon you feel yourself slipping into a state of compete deep inner calm.

Visualize your body. See it vibrating with white healing light.

The brilliant, powerful, and healing light is permeating you from head to toe. Breathe and concentrate on expanding this light.

With each breath the light magnifies tenfold and grows stronger.

You carry this light with you wherever you go.

Visualize yourself upon awakening, at the beginning of your day.

Your body is glowing with the white healing light.

See yourself going to work.

No matter who you meet and what environment you are in, the white light is ever present and overpowers any negative energy that you encounter.

See the people you meet.

When you shake someone's hand, your light expands and envelops them.

They catch a sparkle of your healing light that expands to their body.

Now their energy field is healthy, happy and bright like yours.

Go thru your entire day while sharing the white light of love, healing and protection.

Be aware of this power when you are in any and all circumstances.

How does that affect your day?

Do you feel more protected, powerful, energized and happy?

Upon returning home at the end of the day, observe your energy level.

No matter how much light you gave to everyone you encountered, your light is not depleted, but magnified.

You are the generator of this healing light that can heal everything and everyone.

Breathe and enjoy the consciously reawakened and activated power within you.

AFFIRMATION
**"My body has mastered self-healing.
Any unhealthy disharmony within my body disappears
and is replaced with powerful white healing light.
I am healthy."**

JOURNAL

Note how you feel about your overall self-healing capacity.

Do you feel your body is strong?

Practice the exercise in this chapter and note how you feel afterwards.

Continue with this visualization for a few days, and honestly note how it has affected your overall feeling and well being.

Be firm, disciplined, and persistent in this visualization and do not let any doubts enter your mind. You have this God given self-healing power and must use it.

Make notes and observe the difference when using this exercise and when you lead your life with your usual attitude towards your body, health and wellness.

PART NINE

Protection of Your MIND

44. PROTECTION FROM NEGATIVE THOUGHTS

Our mind attracts what we subconsciously choose.

But you can learn to consciously select your thought patters and protect your mind from negativity, fear and mental stress. By being in charge and learning how to control your thinking patterns and habits, you become the one in charge of your life. You free your mind of negativity and feelings of helplessness, and can enjoy inner peace.

We have all experienced a spell of bad mood. You wake up, and are overwhelmed with problems that need solving. When you've had a challenging situation with your job, or a difficult day at home, you may struggle to find anything positive about your work, appearance, or life in general. Maybe an unfortunate event or series of discouraging experiences propel you towards a negative frame of mind. Persistent long term challenging circumstances leave their imprint on your overall disposition. It is understandable.

Nothing seems to get going the way you want to and sooner or later you succumb to lower and lesser enthusiasm about life in general.

Such an experience can lead to depression, and if we do not make an effort to change our state of mind, we may suffer from chronic depressive states.

Before your mind wonders off into the negative zone, you can prevent it from going any further and really dragging you down.

To be cheerful, positive and inspired despite ongoing challenging circumstances, does take some work.

You can recognize these symptoms and first signs of depression, stop your negative inner dialogue in its tracks, and change the unproductive mind pattern. Protect yourself from negative thoughts entering and expanding in your mind.

Be honest with yourself and reflect if you are the source of negativity, before you blame someone else. Sometimes all you need is some rest and peaceful time by yourself. No pressure, no questions, and no one to answer to, just yourself.

Instead of getting upset with yourself about feeling negative, immediately take a few minutes, practice this exercise and benefit from the positive results.

INNER CONVERSATION

"No matter how upset I feel, I am grateful for all the great blessings in my life. I choose to remain positive and enjoy life. I am open to happy, uplifting energy and people that come into my life. I am protected from negative thoughts and am attracting and creating space for happiness and joy."

EXERCISE

Find a quiet and peaceful place. Relax, sit comfortably and concentrate on your breathing. Inhale and exhale deeply and slowly thru your nose.

For release and elimination of negativity breathing is essential.

Each time you exhale, you feel yourself relaxing deeper and deeper until you enter a state of profound inner calm. Still your mind by listening to your breath. Allow no other thoughts, just the soothing sound of your breath. Every time your mind attempts to go in other directions, bring it gently back to the breath. Be patient with yourself and your mind. Just breathe.

Visualize yourself in a small village. There is no one in sight and the village seems completely empty. Despite dreary, chilly and foggy weather you decide to take a short walk. Almost immediately you find yourself in front of an old door of a large tower. You enter and see a lovely golden staircase. You start walking upward and note that the tower has many beautifully ornamented windows. Every time you pass a window and look out, you notice how the weather is getting nicer, the fog is clearing and the sun is starting to shine. Continue on your walk and soon you reach the top of the tower. There is a beautiful large terrace and everything is prepared for a celebration. It seems that someone is expected. You enter the terrace. The sun is shinning, beautiful music is playing and the sight and views are breathtakingly beautiful. Three wise men come towards you, they have been waiting for you. They introduce themselves to you and their names are Love, Kindness and Compassion. You sit down with them and have a lovely conversation about life. You don't want to leave; they are fun, full of laughter, joy and happy thoughts. You are transformed. Soon it is time for you to go. Before you depart, they give you these words of advice:

"As long as you remember our names, all will be well in your life.

Just remember to love and be kind to yourself and others. Be happy and compassionate towards all, and remember the blessings you have received. Have no space for anything else in your mind, and peace, protection and prosperity will come your way. Now and always."

Their words of advice resonate in your head as you return to the staircase. When you reach the ground you notice that the day is beautiful. In the village, you notice joyful people everywhere, you hear laughter and celebration. A new day has begun. You know that anything is possible and the world is as it should be.

AFFIRMATION
**"I release and exhale all negativity and make space
for positive thoughts, experiences and people.
I fill my life with love, happiness, compassion and gratitude."**
JOURNAL

Note how you felt before this exercise.

Did your mind wonder in negative thought patterns?

It is important that you don't give any power to that negativity.

Release and exhale it.

Let the emotions come over you without trying to control or analyze them. Just let them go. If you feel anger or sadness, release it with each breath. Gradually after a few minutes you will start feeling better. Each time you deeply exhale, your physical and negative tension has an outlet to leave your body - especially if you consciously direct it to do so. Keep your mind on your breath.

After practicing this exercise, note how you feel about life, yourself and the many blessings that you have. Did your mood improve?

Repeat the positive affirmation and keep it in your mind throughout the day.

Write it down and persistently permeate your thinking patterns with it.

45. PROTECTION IN PHYSICAL DANGER

When you find yourself in a dangerous situation you need to act quickly.
This is not the time for slow evaluation and waiting for the situation to disappear.
What if it persists?
Obviously there are the basic emergency actions you can take, depending on your situation, and keeping a calm and centered mind is of outmost importance.
But what happens if all the usual practical advice makes no difference and you are facing something you never thought about, and have never learned what to do in such a case?
This is the time you are left with your intuition. That inner voice that will advise you to turn left instead of right and help you avoid a catastrophe.
An alert mind can be your life's savior.
Sharp reflexes and intuitive concentration is something that can be developed.
Observe, be alert and prepared. No matter what the situation, when you remain centered and calm, you will diffuse the panic others may experience.
Your calm and confident mindset will influence a positive outcome in a most challenging situation.
Know that everything matters, time is of the essence, and you can't afford to hesitate. Make a choice and go with it. If it seems there is nothing you can do to change the situation except wait, you must create a calm and strong energy field.
How many times have we heard of someone defying all odds and surviving an immensely challenging, dangerous and desperate situation?
Do you think that person gave any time to despair, self-pity, panic and procrastination? Maybe they had an occasional fearful thought, but most likely the person was positive, strong minded, and persistently determined to survive.
No wavering thoughts, shivering fears. They are a survivor by nature. What does that mean? It means they had a focused vision, were in tune with their intuitive survival reflexes, and had a will of iron so that nothing could bring them down, break their spirit or diminish their hope. They believed that they will survive, knew it, and willed it so.
Do you have a strong will power? If you do, you too are a survivor.
With intention, you too can train to empower and strengthen this ability within you.

INNER CONVERSATION
"I will awaken within myself the willpower, wisdom and decisiveness of a survivor.
The power of my mind will protect me."

EXERCISE

Find a calm and peaceful place.

Breathe long, deep and slow and completely relax.

Now you will practice how to behave in a potentially dangerous situation.

Visualize yourself crossing the street.

You know this crossway and have crossed it a many times. You take a quick look and decide to cross over. But, there is a split second of time where you feel uneasy, almost like "a shiver thru your spine like" feeling.

Do you pay attention to this inner warning and stop, turn and look again, or do you disregard it and continue? Suddenly you notice a car driving thru a red light. The car is coming towards you and although everything is happening fast, it feels like time is standing still.

What do you do? Stand still in shock and wait for the seemingly inevitable?

Or do you become alert and in this tiny and crucial time capsule manage to move away from the line of fire, and avoid the car?

Is your tendency going to be to stand still and give into the vastness of this possible accident, while helplessly and passively waiting for it to happen?

Now practice seeing yourself in slow motion in that timeless moment while you successfully avoid the car and remain untouched.

Your mind was alert and you heard you intuition that guided you to safety.

Visualize another possible situation or maybe revisit an experience you went thru. Did you take advantage of that split second where a decision was made and your mind and will power influenced the situation?

If not, relive it and practice coming out of it well and untouched.

You may not be able to always avoid every single accident or dangerous situation that comes your way. But, by mindfully willing the best outcome when you find yourself challenged will prove crucially helpful. Do not underestimate your willpower and remember that time does seem to stand still in those moments. And that moment of standstill in this time and space capsule is your opportunity to take charge and save your life.

AFFIRMATION

Here are a few choices for affirmations you may use during a dangerous situation. Choose to memorize and use in visualizations the one that appeals to you most.

"I am creating a white wall (white light, ball, or bubble) of divine protection. I am safe. I am protected. I am well. I am healthy. I am unharmed. "

JOURNAL

Note a dangerous situation that you experienced.

Explore different outcomes had you reacted differently and taken the opportunity of mindfully will and change the scenario. Learn from the experience and release all past regret you may carry with you in connection with such situations. You did the best you could at that time. Next time you will be stronger and wiser. This is a great exercise to test your intuitive reaction when presented with different potentially dangerous scenarios. Make sure you always visualize yourself healthy, untouched, protected, and well. Concentrate on your will power, your strength, and calm wisdom that help you make the best choices. Do not dwell extensively on possible negative outcome. Just practice strong firm willpower and determined mindset to safely emerge from any danger.

Note how that has positively changed and affected your life.

46. ERASE SELF SABOTAGE

We know what is good for us. We know what we should avoid.
Yet there comes a time where all that knowledge means nothing.
We ignore the inner voce and head straight for disaster.
While we ignore the real reason for our desperate behavior, the bad habit or self destructive tendency can take over our life. Embarrassed by the hopelessness of the situation, we tend to ignore it, hide it and deny it.
Anything but to admit it, and face the truth.
What is the truth? That we are afraid, unhappy, have low self-esteem, and are desperately and unsuccessfully trying to fill an emotional void?
Nothing will replace self-love and self-respect, no distracting unproductive behavior, mindless activity and mind altering drug.
It is your mind that is weak, and your weakness is affecting your body and spirit.
Maybe for a time there will be no big visible signs, but after a while of continuously living in ignorance of your inner pain and weakened mind, your entire life will come to an abrupt stop.
Your body will rebel, your spirit will cry, and your mind will deteriorate.
You must remain a watchful guard and protector of your mind.
Do not allow others to make decisions for you, and influence your life to such an extend that you are completely lost.
Do not seek companionship in drugs only to escape your true feelings and inner fears. Is it harmless fun, or is it you running away from the inner you?
Remember who you are, a child of God, with all the rights to happiness, prosperity and divine protection. You are never alone, and no matter what feelings of desperation bring you to the edge, it is never too late to stretch your hand and grab the last branch offered to you and pull yourself from the deep dark canyon you are in. If you do not, there is a long way down and the fall will be deadly.
Get yourself together, prepare for the battle of your life, and defeat the voice of weakness that wants to rule your life.
Yes, you can and you will persevere. You will achieve and live your dream.
For you always have the promise of protection of the divine power.
But listen you must, and remember that you are loved more than is imaginable now and always. You are never ever alone or forgotten.
And that's a message from above. Hear it, feel it, and breathe with it.

INNER CONVERSATION
"I am ready to stand up for myself and be the warrior and protector or my body, mind, and spirit. No harm can come to me, for I will it so."

EXERCISE

Find a peaceful and calm place. Breathe long, deep, and slow and completely relax. With each breath you are sensing your body slipping into a state of deep relaxation.

Visualize yourself in a challenging and tempting situation.

Maybe someone is seducing you with something that is destructive for you.

Or it is just you on your own that is heading for trouble.

You know without a doubt, this is a bad idea.

You know you should stay out of it, and immediately leave or say no.

But you hear a tiny voice that tells you:" Do it. It's nothing. You won't get caught. No one will see. You can handle it."

It is almost like there is another person inside your head, encouraging you to be bad.

Visualize a tiny dwarf. He is the size of a stamp. He is sitting in your ear and it is his voice you are hearing. Usually dwarfs are loving darling creatures, but this dwarf is cranky and moody; he has nothing positive to say to you. He is bad.

He gets into trouble and feels lonely; he wants a companion so he won't feel so alone when he is being bad. So he decides to sit in your ear and listen to your thoughts. He senses that you are a bit reluctant about listening to the protective voice of your intuition. As a matter of fact, you are a bit weak and easy to sway. It does not sound like you care about yourself too much, and he feels that you have no love for yourself. What a prefect scenario for him. First opportunity he gets, he whispers into your ear to seduce you into something unhealthy and dangerous, and self-destructive.

He is the embodiment of your insecurity. The bigger your insecurity, the louder he speaks. The more you want to avoid your inner voice, the bossier he gets until he takes over completely. He makes decisions and choices as he wants.

You need to take back the control of your mind. You are in charge and no one else. See the dwarf getting smaller and smaller. Shrink him into nothingness.

His voice is getting tiny and you can barely hear him. Make him disappear.

Now he is gone. You know the control you have over him and your vices. Your security is back, your love for life is back and you are listening only to yourself.

AFFIRMATION
"I will take charge and listen only to my wise and loving voice of intuition. I love and respect myself now and always."

JOURNAL

Note your challenging self destructive tendencies.

Make a list and honestly observe why you allow each one of these habits to rule your life. Is it loneliness, low self-esteem, feelings of boredom or deep unhappiness?

What emotion are you replacing with your behavior?

What can you consciously do to change that?

What would you need to hear, see or experience to discontinue on your self-destructive path? Are you sabotaging yourself consciously? Most likely not.

Create a list and make a plan for filling these voids in your life.

It should not be up to others, or what you expect from someone else.

Nobody else can fill your voids but you. Nobody is going to make you happy, if you are unhappy in your core. Nobody is going to improve you, if you don't want to improve yourself. Practice the exercise and note how the visualization affected you. Do you believe you are strong enough to conquer your bad tendency?

If not, where can you get help? What or who is holding you back? Learn to be happy and joyful within yourself, and to respect and love yourself. Others will follow, for you will be setting an example of how you want to be treated and who you are. Are you ready to be good, respectful, kind, and loving towards yourself?

47. ATTRACTING PROTECTION

Once you've empowered your body's energy shield you are ready to create a bigger protection space all round you.

It is essential that you create a safe and peaceful environment in your home. But keeping that self - protecting energy with you throughout the day, expanding it and attracting positive, kind people into your life is another matter.

You aura may not be seen with untrained eyes, but it can be felt. Your personal magnetism affects everyone around you. Magnetism is closely connected to your aura's vibration level. If your etheric filed is strong and expanded, people sensitive and receptive to that energy and vibration will be affected by it and attracted to you. Like attracts like. It is imperative for your own well being and safety to be in charge of your state of mind and know your strengths and weaknesses. When you are filled with fears and doubts, take time for yourself to recharge and improve your mindset. It is wiser to emerge into the world with a positive and confident mindset as opposed to vulnerable and unprotected.

We've all experienced an energy shift when someone with a large presence walks into a room. Everyone turns around and notices them, subconsciously feeling their energy. The entire room is instantly transformed, new energy connecting and merging. You may not be aware of it, but it is the person's vibration that has startled you and made you notice them. If the vibration is magnetically positive and compatible with yours, you will feel an attraction, a pull to meet and communicate with them. You'll want to be in that energy field. If you want to connect with and be surrounded with spiritually abundant souls, you must first project that energy yourself. Be confident and know who you are, define yourself and face the world self assured and ready for equal exchange. Create a balance of give and take.

If you are frightened, depleted, lonely and needy and looking for someone to help you find yourself, you will find an appropriate match. Do not fool yourself thinking that in such a case, you will get what you need at no cost.

There will be a lesson in every circumstance, especially when unbalanced.

It may appear as if the person has aided you in self-discovery, but they also needed your dependent energy. They felt stronger themselves by helping a person like you…weak and insecure. The dynamic shifts when you become your true strong self. Now this person is out of a" job". If you desire to attract an honest and giving person, make sure that deep in your soul you are coming from the same position. If you are defining yourself and finding your calling, be open to guiding forces. Know who you are what you want, for it is of the greatest importance. Do you know and like yourself? Can you imagine spending time with you? If you can't stand the thought of being alone, why would you imagine you are such tremendous fun for someone else? When you get to know yourself and like yourself, you are in the right place to attract an equally content and self-sufficient soul as yourself. Otherwise there will be an energy imbalance. It will take work to create harmony. And your relationships with friends, lovers, the people you spend time or share your life with should not be about working hard. It should feel and be easy, always evolving, harmonious and peaceful. Only then can your electromagnetic protection field merge with the one of your chosen companion, and together you become unbeatable and invincible.

INNER CONVERSATION
"I am confident and secure with my own power.
I am ready to open up and attract souls alike
that will help me grow, love and prosper.
Together we will co create and expand a safe and peaceful energy filed".

EXERCISE
Find a quiet and peaceful place. Breathe long, deep and slow and completely relax. With each deep breath you are relaxing deeper and deeper until you enter a state of deep inner peace and calm
Visualize the ocean. It is wild and powerful.
The silver, blue colors are twinkling in the sunlight and the sky's perfect pale blue colors offer you a sight of otherworldly beauty.
You are swimming in this ocean. It feels wonderful and invigorating.
You are swimming far away from the shore and are aware there might be danger nearby. Suddenly your fearful thoughts attract a dangerous being.
A large shark is approaching towards you and there is no place to hide, no time for escape and the situation looks hopeless.
You center your mind and visualize your friends – the dolphins. You call them with your mind and within seconds they appear at your side. The vast number of them frightens the shark away and he is gone as fast as he appeared. Your friends- the dolphins- stay with you at your side until you reach the shore safely. With their high pitched frequency sound they communicate to you their undeniable love and loyalty. They promise they will always be there to help you and protect you. You will do the same for them.
Whenever you can, you will help elevate the people's awareness about dolphins and the need for their preservation and protection. By attracting each other into your life with positive intentions you have magnified the protection field for all.

AFFIRMATION

"I attract protection thru creatures and people that I meet and circumstances that I encounter. They guide and help me stay safe. Together we magnify and expand our field of protection."

JOURNAL

Note what people you attract into your life.

Are they unconditionally protective of you?

Are they reliable and loving?

What do you offer them?

Would you like to increase your circle of trustworthy friends?

What do you consider a sign of loyalty in friendship?

Note how this exercise expands your mind awareness about protection.

Have you missed offered opportunities of protection?

What can you do in the future to increase your awareness of help and protection the universe sends your way?

48. YOU ARE IN CHARGE

How many times have you blamed others for some unfortunate event that happened or a situation that seemed to take everything out of control?

How did you behave? Did you remain calm and confident in the eyes of the storm or did you allow yourself to be helplessly dragged around like a piece of paper in the wind?

It is much easier to blame the circumstances or others than to face yourself and the facts: you lost control of your mind. You did not know right from wrong, left from right and where to go, what to do. This is not meant to scold you or make you feel bad, but only to remind you to use what has been given to you.

The power of your mind. An immeasurable power that you have yet to realize. In the future, humans will pay more attention to that power.

The distance of time and space becomes meaningless if your mind can cross all that. The outcome of an event, the message you want to convey to someone without the help of telephone or internet.

How do you envision controlling your thoughts and mastering such communication, if you can barely master and control your mind in your every day life? That means we have a lot of work to do, a lot of practice.

It requires inner work, facing yourself and your doubts, demands and fears that prevent you from holding your mind sturdy and strong.

There is no better time than now to take charge.

Before you can talk to your spirit, you must still the mind. Only then can you listen to your inner voice. You may be able to do it in a quiet safety of your home, but what about when you re-enter the world of noise, visual distractions and other people's thoughts and vibrations? Can you hold on to a calm mind then?

That is your next step: Remaining calm and in charge no matter where you are. After you learn to hold still your mind at home, maybe even while dealing with everyday life, in the city, on the bus, at work, while standing in line at the bank, you are ready for the next challenging level.

How about when some drastic event occurs? Can you remain equally calm then? Not indifferent, but very aware, prepared, and yet completely calm?

That is the mastery we must strive towards. It will help us avoid making mistakes, hurt one another, and act by impulse instead of with the power of the mind.

INNER CONVERSATION
"I am aware of the power of my mind.
I will strive to bring self-control and stillness to my mind."

EXERCISE

Find a calm and peaceful place. Breathe long deep and slow and completely relax. Continue breathing and feel how with each breath you are sinking deeper and deeper into a state of complete peace and inner calm.

Visualize the ocean. The sun is setting and the sight is breathtakingly beautiful. You are the captain of a lovely sailboat. You have had it for years and have taken impeccable care of it. The sailboat is your pride and joy. You are sailing out to the sea and enjoying every moment of it. You consider yourself a great captain. You have sailed thru many a storm and always returned to the shore safely.

But you do like to live dangerously. A challenge seems always tempting and today is one of those days. You have heard the reports about the possibility of a storm, but it did not prevent you from your trip. You know this could turn nasty in a matter of minutes, but you secretly like the danger of it.

It is exciting and makes you fell alive.

Suddenly it happens. The expected storm attacks in full fury. The waves are huge, the winds overpowering. Bravely and fearlessly you manage to keep everything under control and stay on board. Out of nowhere an enormous wave comes over the edge and sweeps you off the boat and throws you into the ocean. It is scary, and dangerous. You are alone, so no one can help you. There is a safety rope hanging over the edge of the deck and you manage to catch it. With all your might you hold on to the rope. The sailboat is out of control, with no one guiding and navigating it. This goes on for what seems like eternity and you feel your body getting weak. But your mind is determined that you will master the situation and with what seems the last strength you manage to pull yourself back on the sailboat and take charge. As soon as you're back the storm is letting down and soon the waters are calm again. An intense stillness takes over the ocean and although you feel like you went thru a war, you are navigating the sailboat back to the shore safely. You managed to keep it under control even when everything seemed to be going wrong. You know that you will always be the one in charge of your sails. No matter how strong the wind, how wild the storm, you are the captain of this ship and will always be. You are the boss.

Visualize yourself reaching the shore safely and smile.

You have made it once again.

The sailboat is like your mind, ever restless and unpredictable. But even when outside elements throw havoc in the sails of your mind, you manage to hold on and survive.

Pay attention and know that you-the captain, are stirring the ship and the waters are calm again. Just pay attention to where you want to sail.

Carry with you that vision of the sailboat and know that you will always be the one in charge of your mind.

AFFIRMATION
**"No matter what winds of life grab a hold of my sails,
I remain calm and determined to sail home.
My mind is steady."**

JOURNAL

Note how that visualization affected you.

Could you relate to the captain and his determination?

Would you act similarly and remain confident of your survival?

Find a similar situation in your life. Perhaps an emotional situation that takes hold of you and brings you inner unrest- a storm. Can you hold on to and remember whose boat you are sailing-whose mind this is affecting? It is your mind and as much as it seems impossible you will keep control of it and stay strong.

Visualize yourself remaining strong thru the storms and challenges life presents to you and know you are in charge of your mind.

Note how this awareness reduces your feelings of helplessness and reawakens your capacity to control your mind.

Note how this attitude affects your future and self-confidence so that you can and will successfully master your mind thru any challenge.

PART TEN

Protection of Your SOUL

49. YOUR SOUL KNOWS THE ANSWER

Yes, you hold all the answers to all your questions within your soul.
Intuitively you know all you will ever need and want to know.
When you meet someone and fall in love, somewhere deep inside your soul, you un-mistakenly know this is the right person for you.
It is not necessarily words you hear, but there is an all-knowing feeling that permeates your being with complete certainly.
Just like you know that something is going to happen at a certain time, or someone will call you. You know it deep inside your soul.
These premonitions or awareness of an event before is going to happen are messages from your higher consciousness which activates and works with your extra sensory perception. If you decide to pay attention to them, your life will become more fruitful, interesting, uplifting, and happy.
Most of all, you will live in perfect synchronicity with your spirit. A sense of inner contentment and being in the right place at the right time with the right person will prevail. And that is reason enough to pay attention.
Most of our disharmonies and unhappiness in life occurs when we separate ourselves and ignore the deep knowledge within our soul.
We go against it out of fear, material insecurity, low self-esteem and deep rooted doubts. We doubt in the power and immortality of our spirit. We try desperately to decide and control everything with our mind, barely listening to our heart and forgetting our spirit.
But sooner or later, the life's journey will bring us back to the beginning of the road. We have to know ourselves, search deep within and acknowledge the deep inner source of power that is available to us at all times.
Awaken the inner knowledge and remember your soul is untouchable, indestructible and immortal.
Connect your life's journey in this world with your soul's knowledge from universal consciousness, and expand your horizon beyond the stars in the sky.
It is all there for you. Be, trust, enjoy and know that your higher spirit will guide you.

INNER CONVERSATION
"I know my soul is a part of Divine everlasting power.
I will reawaken the awareness and knowledge of my spirit."

EXERCISE

Find a peacefully and quiet place. Breathe long, deep, and slow and completely relax and let go. Continue breathing and with each breath relax deeper and deeper into a state of complete serenity and peace.

Visualize an old country road. You know this road and have traveled here before. It is the road that leads to your home. But it also connects you to many different places. Actually you can get to anywhere in the word from this road.

But you are familiar only with the last part of the road, the part that is close to your home where you return each night to rest.

Every day, you wake up with the desire to walk the road and see where it will take you. There are so many places to explore, see and meet others.

You have met friends, lovers, enemies, had happy, challenging and enlightening experiences all staring with the journey on this road. But no matter what happened, you always found the correct way back home.

It is morning now and you are leaving home, on your way to a new experience. You do not know where you are going, or whom you will meet, and what will happen today.

You have an idea, but every time you make a plan and have certain expectations, it all changes and nothing ever goes the way you expected it.

So this day will be a surprise again. As you are walking, you suddenly notice the road has a fork. Which way to go?

There is an olive tree by the left side of the road. The tree is old and sturdy and has seen many storms. You decide to sit under this tree and rest for a while. The moment you sit under the tree, you know this is the direction in the road you must take. It is as if the tree has given you an unspoken signal. You know without a doubt in your mind that the tree is your protector. Every day when you travel the road, you meet this tree at a different place. Wherever there is a fork in the road or intersection, this tree is there. And every time you decide to sit underneath it, it reveals to you where you must travel.

The tree is your sturdy companion and even though it doesn't seem to be able to move, it does, and it doesn't seem to be able to talk, but it sends you messages, and it seems it can not offer you anything but shade, but it offers you protection and advice.

When you return from your journey tonight, the tree will be standing near your home, as it has been forever and a day.

This is your spirit guide, always with you.

AFFIRMATION
**"I will open my inner vision and find my spirit guides.
I will pay attention to the protection, guidance,
wisdom and comfort they offer me."**

JOURNAL
Note how you feel about your spirit guides before this experience.
Have you ever thought about or desired to find them?
Do you believe in them?
Have you ever had the feeling an unseen force was guiding you, protecting you
and taking you in the right direction?
Note all that comes to mind without too much analyzing or searching for logical
explanations.
How did this exercise affect your openness to spirit guides?
Pay attention in the next couple of days to everything that influences and affects
your decision-making.
Search your soul and see if you can discover your spirit guides in your life.

50. YOUR INDESTRUCTIBLE SOUL SPEAKS

The voice from within. How often do we hear about this inner voice?
The voice of the soul. We all have it, but do we listen? Many times when a challenging situation presents itself to us, we know deep inside, that there was a moment in time, when we heard that warning voice, that alarm bell, that siren that was desperately trying to wake us up, warn us, and prevent us from making a big mistake. It did everything it could to protect us from the pain that followed.
The only thing this voice can not make us do, is listen.
If we don't listen, nothing can be done.
It is like when you watch a child run towards a hot plate. You are screaming to stop them, but they don't listen, they have to go and touch it. And eventually get burned. That is what happens to us. We get burned. And in that instant when it happens, we know. " Ah, I did hear that small voice tell me to watch out, I did hear it, I knew it, but I didn't listen."
And so the child will know next time not to touch the plate and we will know next time to listen to that inner voice. Or will we?
When we refuse to hear the spirit voice, it may try to reach us in other ways. Like thru a song on the radio. You will turn it on and the words in the lyrics you hear are the exact answers to your questions. Has that ever happened to you?
But still you may doubt it. "It can't be true" you will think. Until you meet a friend and without a singular clue, he will tell you a piece of advice that makes no sense to them, but it does to you. It is the second warning you've received now.
But will you listen? Maybe. And then again maybe you will get lucky and the sprit will try to make you listen one last time, and you will finally get the message.
"It is just too many coincidences" you will say. But you know there isn't such a thing as a coincidence. It is a part of perfectly designed plan. A plan so perfect that even in your wildest dreams you could not come up with it.
When your own plan seems crushed and your dreams destroyed, you receive a sudden surprise. The course of events take a sudden turn and your dream is realized, but not the way you envisioned it.
Much better. It is as if our dreams outdid themselves.
Trust and listen. Your soul knows and has lots to tell you.
When? How about right now. When you are truly ready, you will hear the answer.

INNER CONVERSATION
"I know my soul carries the information from my deep past.
I will listen and learn."

EXERCISE

Find a peaceful and quiet place. Breathe long deep and slow and completely relax. With each breath you feel yourself sinking deeper and deeper into deep state of inner peace.

Visualize yourself on a beautiful, endless grass meadow.

The day is bright and you are enjoying the lovely sight.

Breathe in the fresh air and completely relax.

In the far distance you notice a horse.

The beautiful animal is running towards you.

Powerful, majestic and fast. Someone is ridding this horse, but you can't quite see who. The horse is approaching and suddenly it is standing in front of you. An angelic being is riding this horse.

This being is smiling at you and looking at you with loving, all knowing eyes.

"Who are you?" you ask.

"I am the voice of your soul. I can transform into anything you desire, today I appeared as an angel like you wished. You called me and here I am."

The being is looking at you, serene and otherworldly. The wind is blowing.

"I don't remember calling you. But I am happy that you are here and I can see you. Do you have anything to tell me?" you continue.

"Oh, yes, I have the answers to all the questions that you long for. Ask me anything you want."

The being is smiling at you and patiently waiting.

"How can I expand my mind to have all the knowledge that you have?" you ask.

"There are no limits to your mind, only the ones you created," the angel answers.

The wind is getting stronger and the horse is growing restless.

"Will all my dreams come thru?" you inquire.

"Only if you will share your blessings with others and help bring peace to this world.". The horse turns around and starts to take the angel away.

"When can I speak to you again? There are so many things I want to know, so many questions that I have" you ask.

Before the angel leaves, the horse turns back for a moment, and the angel looks deeply into your eyes and says:

"I am with you, every moment of your life, I cry your tears and know your dreams, I protect you in need and carry you in sorrow, I remind you now and always that you are never alone and are loved deeply and profoundly, more than you will ever know".

The angel smiles at you one more time with deep love and care, and disappears into the horizon in an instant.

You feel serene, at peace and very much loved.

AFFIRMATION
**"I can hear the guiding voice of my soul at any given moment.
It is filled with love for me and every living creature if this world."**

JOURNAL

Note how did this visualization journey make you feel.

Has it helped you open the boundaries of your mind and expand beyond the limitations you have set?

Have you ever thought to put a visual picture to your soul?

Does it help you feel more comfort and care knowing that you may speak to your higher-self any time you so desire?

Repeat this exercise in a few weeks and spend more time talking to your angelic inner being.

Note what other question spontaneously come to mind and what answers you hear.

Observe how this exercise expands your awareness and helps you reconnect and communicate with your soul power.

51. YOUR SOUL LOVES UNCONDITIONALLY

Love lives on forever. It knows no boundaries of place, time and space.
Falling in love with someone in an instant sounds impossible. But it happens, hopefully to every one of us. You have known them before in another place and time and are reconnecting with them again. The feeling that you've known each other forever is real. You have. The soul of your loved one is forever engraved in your soul. He/she is your twin flame.

How do you recognize the love of your life? When the time is right, he will come your way and there will be no doubt about it. Sometimes it can happen that your true love has been in front of you for years, but you have been too busy to notice it. Maybe your best friend, that saw you thru a few brokenhearted experiences and love affairs is your true love. Always reliable and lovingly kind, and after years you realize he is the one. Anything is possible, as love has many unexpected faces. You can not plan to fall in love. You are unique and your love story is one of a kind. Maybe everyone around you has already found his or her true love and you are still searching. You are starting to loose hope and think you will never be blessed with true love. But do not despair. It is never ever too late to fall in love and when the time is perfect your love will appear. There is also the possibility that you have a few different loves to experience in this lifetime. Your first love will transform your life, but the person may be completely inappropriate for you twenty years from now.

One of the true challenges in love is to grow thru life's changes and stay connected and compatible. Usually one of the partners stirs in a different direction and the lover left behind simply can not catch up and feel comfortable with a new person that is evolving in front of their eyes. Some of us have large transformations in life and others sail a smooth even ride. It is difficult to balance the growing life-experiences and always feel on the same wavelength. Communication can be a great savior. Awareness that we all do change and grow daily is important. We must be protective of our relationship and do not let too many outsiders into that intimate atmosphere.

Anyone else will give you an opinion that reflects their personal experience that may be very different from yours, and can contain different outcome. Only the two people in the relationship know what exactly is going on in the relationship. Once you have found the love of your life, do everything you can to hold on to it, cherish and nurture it so you can make it grow, expand and last forever and a day. If your paths separate, remain faithful that a new companion, new love will find you when destiny plays out. If your true love has left you behind, remember they are always with you in spirit, and one day you will rejoice and meet again.

INNER CONVERSATION
"I am open to life's adventurous plan for my heart. I will pay attention and not carry pre-conceived ideas that may make me miss my eternal flame."

EXERCISE
Find a peaceful and quiet place. Breathe long deep and slow and completely relax. With every breath you are sinking into a deep state of relaxation and peace.

Visualize yourself sitting at the edge of a lake. The place around the lake is very special. It is a bird sanctuary. There are many different kinds of birds and the sight is truly magical. There are small, colorful, large and lanky birds, unusual shapes and sizes of birds, you are observing them and enjoying the sight. All birds seem to be coupled. The pairs are never far apart, always keeping a loving and caring eye on each other.

They are flying nearby and enjoying the serenity of this place. Suddenly you notice one lonely bird. This very unusual exotic bird is sitting on a branch of a small tree and watching everything from a distance. It looks lonely and yet absolutely lovely. There is something about it that attracts you instantly to it. Its calmness, and distance from the crowd, the watchful eye and sweet patient disposition are very endearing. Suddenly the bird disappears. Where did it go? You are somehow sorry you did not get a closer look at this lovely bird. As much as there are many fascinating and seemingly more interesting looking birds around you, the one that's on your mind is this one.

And then you notice it did not fly away. It simply changed the three that it was sitting on. Now it is sitting much closer to you. You can see it better and you notice the sparkling eyes. This bird has something very special and you do not know what exactly it is, but you can not take your eyes away from it. It has you mesmerized. You need to get closer to it and see if you can somehow communicate with it. The bird notices you. It has been watching you from afar. You are the reason it came closer. It wants to take a closer look. Interesting. What is it about this bird? You don't understand. It makes no sense. You usually like big, white birds and yet you can not look at anything else but this exotic unique creature. You decide you will get closer. You stand up and spread your wings and fly to it. You see, you are a bird as well, and look precisely like this unique bird. You two are alike in every possible way, perfectly matched. àYou've found your true love.

AFFIRMATION
**"I will keep my eyes and heart open for my endless love of my soul.
I will keep the flame alive for the eternal
and unconditional loves of my life."**

JOURNAL

Note the way you feel about finding your true love.

If you have a love in your life, remember how you felt the first time you met.

Was there a feeling of old connection?

Was there an illogical-not my type-feeling?

What are the qualities that attract you to this person?

If you are waiting for your true love, what are your expectations?

Is it possible you let others influence whom you should have as a partner?

Be honest and ask yourself, what is the single most important aspect you desire for in your partner? Why is that important to you?

What do you have to offer them?

Do you believe in soul mates- twin flames?

Repeat this exercise in a few weeks and note how it has opened your awareness and expanded your restricted vision and openness to meeting your mate where you least expect it.

If you have found your love, revisit the qualities that touched your soul.

Remember the first essential attraction and dynamic of your relationship and expand the meaning of all little things that meant so much.

Breathe and trust in the divine plan.

52. YOUR IMMORTAL SOUL TRANSCENDS TIME

Life. You wonder what it's all about. All the hard work, effort, pain, sorrow, love and glory, sometimes it seems like a dream. Wasn't it just yesterday you were a child in school? And then your teenage years went by in a snap. Before you really knew what hit you, here you are all grown up. Hopefully. And now, more than ever you wonder what life is all about. You may have different views, explanations of life and death, rationalizations of why and when, and it is working for you to a certain degree. But if you would look behind the secret curtain on the stage of life, what would you find? The greatest mysteries of life can be unraveled when you discover yourself and the mystery of you.

Look at your life as an adventure, a beautiful journey. Quantity is not as important as is the quality and intention of your life. Those are the things that seem lost in today's world; yet those are the ones that count.

Your intentions and actions stay with you and travel with your soul.
Wherever you go, your unique energy and soul information comes along.
Why do you feel so comfortable in a certain country and not in another?
Why do you feel an attraction to someone you've never met before?
Or have you met before? You feel like you know them.
Why are you so familiar with certain activities, as if you would have done them a million times before? Have you been here before? You think about it and decide. You don't have to tell everyone in the world; your experiences and beliefs are your very own. Your treasure chest.

Some have a habit to talk about everything and talking is good. But feeling is even more important. Are you talking so you would not have to feel? Silence and inner search are as important for your survival as is food, air and the sun.

No matter how isolated you feel, deep inside your soul you know you are never alone. You are protected and your soul is untouchable. Your essence is eternal. It travels thru time, thru lifetimes and carries within energies, emotions and vibrations that make you unique. What joy to be a part of something so powerful and ever present. Do not mistake this life for reality. It is all a wonderful dream where all things are possible. Make the very best of it and know that the spiritual protection shield is impenetrable and ever present. Trust and let go. Let the forces take you to the next stop on your journey. Believe and know that the universal plan for you is much more glorious than you could have ever planned or imagined yourself.

INNER CONVERSATION
"I will remember my essence and my soul's journey.
I will reconnect to the universal power that is ever present and enjoy the especially created space for my soul in this universal plan of creation."

EXERCISE

Find a quiet and peaceful place. Relax and be still.
Concentrate on your long, deep, and slow breath.
Visualize yourself in a time capsule. It looks like a small plane or spaceship.
There is space for only one person - you. You are sitting comfortably in the only
passenger seat and enjoying a spectacular view. The craft has an automatic
navigation system, so you can relax and let yourself go. You are flying thru the
galaxies of all amazing otherworldly colors. The journey is fascinating, exciting,
hypnotic and very real. You especially like the galaxy you are approaching now.
You notice a beautiful small planet. There are rainbow colors surrounding it and
you hear beautiful music in the distance. You decide to land and take a look.
As fast as your wish crosses your mind, the craft starts descending.
You are coming closer and closer to this planet. You land on the ground with
ease. The beings of this planet look human and they welcome you with love.
An instant family is given to you and your life experience on this planet begins.
You meet a lot of old friends, some old acquaintances that you don't like, and a
few people you love dearly. You forget about the spacecraft and your journey.
You are immersed into this life. It is fun, it is exciting, and it is pain and lessons.
It is also love. When you finish your experience, you decide to return back to your
spaceship. You take a rest and reflect on your experience. Then you move on
and fly thru new galaxies and worlds. You might land in another world, another
planet. This is your soul's journey. Wherever you stop, there are always
interesting adventures, people, and loves that you find. The more you
travel, the wiser you become and sometimes you remember your origins.
It seems like a distant fog, but you subconsciously know about it.
You are catching on to the game.
So where is your home? Everywhere and nowhere. Who is your family?
Everyone and no one. Who do you love? All. What time is it? There is no time.
When you so desire, you ask the automatic pilot to take you back to your source.
Instantly you find yourself in a world more beautiful, extraordinarily colorful, and
majestic than any you've ever seen before.
This is your home. Everyone is here; there is glorious music, beauty and nature
all around you. All the people you love and adore are right here with you.
There is no lack of anything. There is only love, peace, and abundance of beauty.
This is your essence, your true home. You may return anytime and replenish your
soul with love and light. Remember wherever you are on your particular journey,
whatever your challenges, suffering and lessons, you have a home richer than
anything you've ever imagined, a family that loves you unconditionally, and you
are watched over every second of your existence. But then again, seconds don't
exist. There is only eternity. You've been a man, a woman, lived as a part of all
races and cultures, and you have journeyed thru time and experienced all variety

of lifetimes. You know the equality and nature of all souls. You know about life. You know we are all connected with life force now, thru eternity. Practice this journey when you need to feel reassurance, connection, purpose and a sense of belonging in your life. It will help you transform your challenging feelings, and remember that you are and always will be surrounded with immeasurable love.

AFFIRMATION
"I accept and appreciate all forms of life.
I know I am connected and a part of all living creatures, big and small.
My soul is but a drop in the ocean of life.
I dance, love, and make music with the waves.
I taste the exquisite variety of life and make the world complete.
I remember my spiritual protection field."

JOURNAL
Note your feelings about your place of origin.
Do you believe in eternal life of your soul? Do you feel connected to all life?
What is your contribution to this world? Can you try to see this life as an adventure? Note all feelings and questions that this exercise brings to your mind. Reflect upon your questions.
Repeat the exercise at a later date and review your views. How have they changed if any, and how has that affected your every day life?

53. YOU ARE ONE WITH THE UNIVERSE

God. A big word and an even bigger meaning. Instead of wondering what religion is the one that holds all the answers and offers eternal life, we should ask ourselves what does that word mean to us?

The vastness and immense power that is divine lives in us all.

We are all connected and one.

When we lose sight of that great power, love and life, we feel divided and lost.

It does not matter who your God is. What matters is that you are aware of the universal divine force that resides in all of us. This power protects and loves you more that you will ever know. The knowledge, wisdom, love and compassion that divine power offers you is indescribable and unimaginable.

Seeing, feeling, hearing and recognizing that power in everything and everyone around us is essential for our spiritual evolution.

We are not enemies, but are all children of God.

We are here together in this world, breathing the same air and drinking the same water. We all feel the sun, rain and hear the thunder.

We are small and vulnerable. We are but sparks of eternal fire of life.

Have you ever looked out of the window while sitting on a plane?

Have you seen your hometown get smaller and smaller, until you saw just a tiny speck of something indescribable? Have you seen the roads and the cars on them disappear? How small are people? Very, very small.

Suddenly your problems seem even smaller.

How can your problems feel overwhelming, if you are so small you can't even see your city, let alone humans from the plane?

Have you noticed the clouds and how gorgeously sunny and clear the sky is above the clouds? Have you seen other planes below and above you and have you felt even smaller?

What matters in a world of these proportions? Your problems, worries, desires, and dreams? Everything matters.

You matter, others matter, clean air and water, and our future matters.

But all that is meaningless if there is no peace.

Peace on earth, peace in all mankind and peace in your heart.

All that is needed to have peace in your soul.

Whatever and whoever your God is, peace, prosperity and protection are the elements we all need, seek and deserve.

God is peace.

INNER CONVERSATION

"I will awaken my ever present connection to the Divine and
share the enlightening love with all beings of this world."

EXERCISE

Find a calm and peaceful place. Breathe long, deep and slow and become completely relaxed. With each breath you experience a deeper and more relaxed state.

Visualize yourself walking in a large garden filled with flowers. They are absolutely mesmerizing. All colors, shapes and sized, one more beautiful than the other. The scent in the air is magical, the breeze is swaying the blooms, and it seems as if they are dancing in the wind.

There is an amazingly unique butterfly that is flying from one flower to the next. You want to follow it. It drinks the nectar from all different blooms and keeps flying in a certain direction. You are following this magical butterfly for a while and eventually it brings you to an ancient building.

It looks like a temple of some kind, from an ancient civilization.

You feel an uncontrollable need to walk up the stairs and enter.

The temple is filed with more wild flowers. They are growing everywhere and the place has a vibration so serene, peaceful and pleasant that you never want to leave. It feels like home.

In the center of this temple burns a powerful flame on an large golden candle.

On it you see inscriptions in many different languages and alphabets.

They all say the same words: God is Peace. There is a lovely golden chair waiting for you to sit on and rest. You take a seat, relax and absorb the beauty around you. The candle keeps burning, you gaze at the flame and suddenly you see a vision of a face in it. You do not know this face. Before you can think of whom it may be, the face changes. Thousands of faces appear, millions even, one after the other, all glowing in this divine eternal flame. For an instant you see your face as well. You remember, deep within your soul, that the universal divine power and you are one.

You stay in the temple for what seems like an eternity.

When you are ready, you depart. You can come back anytime you so desire and replenish your thirst for knowledge, love and enjoy the everlasting peace in the temple of God.

Your God. In your heart and soul.

AFFIRMATION
**"I am one with the Universal power.
There is no end or beginning... only eternity."**

JOURNAL

Note your feelings about God - the universal power before this exercise.
How did you feel in the sacred temple?
Do you have a place in your life where you can go to recharge, and replenish your energy?
If not, create a special place where you can enjoy complete peace.
Make it a priority to visit it regularly and commune with your God.

ABOUT THE AUTHOR

SABRINA MESKO Ph.D.H. is the LA Times and international bestselling author of "Healing Mudras -Yoga for your Hands" by Random House. Her book reached number five on the Los Angeles Times Health Books Bestseller list and is translated into 14 languages. She authored over 20 of books on MUDRAS, MEDITATION and YOGA, including MUDRA THERAPY, POWER MUDRAS and MUDRAS FOR ASTROLOGICAL SIGNS. She produced and directed her Visionary awards finalist double DVD titled: " Chakra Mudras".

Sabrina studied with Master Guru Maya, healing breath techniques with Master Sri Sri Ravi Shankar and completed a four-year study of Paramahansa Yogananda's Kriya Yoga technique. She graduated from the internationally known Yoga College of India and became a certified yoga therapist. An immense interest and study of powerful hand gestures - Mudras, led Sabrina to the world's only Master of White Tantric Yoga, Yogi Bhajan, who entrusted her with the sacred Mudra - hand yoga techniques giving her the responsibility to spread this ancient and powerful knowledge world wide.

Sabrina holds a Bachelors Degree in Sensory Approaches to Healing, a Masters in Holistic Science and a Doctorate in Ancient and Modern Approaches to Healing from the American Institute of Holistic Theology. She is board certified from the American Alternative medical Association and American Holistic Health Association.

Sabrina appeared on The Discovery Channel documentary on hands, the Roseanne Show, CNBC News and numerous international live television programs. Her articles and columns have been published in countless publications. Sabrina has hosted her own weekly TV show about health, well-being and complementary medicine. She is an executive member of the World Yoga Council and has led extensive Teacher Training Yoga Therapy educational programs. She directed and produced her latest interactive double DVD titled " Chakra Mudras" a Visionary awards finalist. Sabrina has also created award winning international Spa and Wellness Centers from concept, architectural planning, equipment and product selection, staff training and unique healing signature Spa treatments. She is a motivational keynote conference speaker addressing large audiences all over the world. Her highly dynamic and engaging approach leaves audiences inspired and uplifted.

Sabrina lives in Los Angeles. For more information about her online personal mentorship Certification courses for MUDRA TEACHER TRAINING, MUDRA THERAPY and ESOTERIC MUDRA METHOD visit her popular website at www.sabrinamesko.com

Made in the USA
Lexington, KY
18 April 2016